YEAR C
ADVENT/CHRISTMAS/EPIPHANY

```
COKESBURY  RALE  34500
12/02/97  09:41  E     6    8482

CHARGE TO ACCOUNT # C451682

DUKE MEMORIAL UN METH CHURCH
504 WEST CHAPEL HILL ST

DURHAM, NC 27701

P.O. # 02

     1 @  12.95 0687338042  0%$    12.95
                  PREACHING REV COM LECT C
     1 @   2.90 SHIP        0%$     2.90
SUBTOTAL                      $    15.85
TAX      @ 6.00%              $     0.95
TOTAL                         $    16.80
TENDERED Charge  C451682      $    16.80


          This is your invoice.
   Please retain to match w/your statement.

   x    Phone - ebs
```

YEAR C
ADVENT/CHRISTMAS/EPIPHANY

PREACHING
THE REVISED
COMMON
LECTIONARY

Marion Soards
Thomas Dozeman
Kendall McCabe

ABINGDON PRESS
Nashville

PREACHING THE REVISED COMMON LECTIONARY
YEAR C: ADVENT/CHRISTMAS/EPIPHANY

Copyright © 1994 by Abingdon Press

This book is printed on recycled, acid-free paper.

Library of Congress Cataloging-in-Publication Data

Soards, Marion L., 1952–
  Preaching the revised common lectionary: year C / Marion Soards, Thomas Dozeman, Kendall McCabe.
      p. cm.
  Includes indexes.
  Contents: [1] Advent/Christmas/Epiphany.
  ISBN **0-687-33804-2** (v. 1: alk. paper)
  1. Lectionary preaching. 2. Bible—Homiletical use. I. Dozeman, Thomas B. II. McCabe, Kendall, 1939– . III. Common lectionary (1992). IV. Title.
BV4235.L43S63   1994   93-30550
251—dc20

You may order the software edition of *Preaching the Revised Common Lectionary,* packaged in Year A, B, or C from your local religious bookstore, or by calling 1-800-672-1789. Specify whether your computer system is running at least DOS 3.0 or Windows.

Scripture quotations, unless otherwise noted, are from the New Revised Standard Version of the Bible, copyright © 1989 by the Division of Christian Education of the National Council of the Churches of Christ in the USA. Used by permission.

97 98 99 00 01 02 03 — 10 9 8 7 6 5 4 3

MANUFACTURED IN THE UNITED STATES OF AMERICA

Contents

CONTENTS

This is one volume in a twelve-volume series. Each volume contains commentary and worship suggestions for a portion of the lectionary cycle A, B, or C. Since the lections for a few special days do not change from one lectionary cycle to another, material for each of these days appears in only one of the volumes. Appropriate cross references in the table of contents lead the reader to material in other volumes of the series.

Introduction

Now pastors and students have a systematic treatment of essential issues of the Christian year and Bible study for worship and proclamation based on the Revised Common Lectionary. Interpretation of the lectionary will separate into three parts: Calendar, Canon, and Celebration. A brief word of introduction will provide helpful guidelines for utilizing this resource in worship through the Christian year.

Calendar. Every season of the Christian year will be introduced with a theological interpretation of its meaning, and how it relates to the overall Christian year. This section will also include specific liturgical suggestions for the season.

Canon. The lectionary passages will be interpreted in terms of their setting, structure, and significance. First, the word *setting* is being used loosely in this commentary to include a range of different contexts in which biblical texts can be interpreted from literary setting to historical or cultic settings. Second, regardless of how the text is approached under the heading of setting, interpretation will always proceed to an analysis of the structure of the text under study. Third, under the heading of significance, central themes and motifs of the passage will be underscored to provide a theological interpretation of the text as a springboard for preaching. Thus interpretation of the lectionary passages will result in the outline on the next page.

Celebration. This section will focus on specific ways of relating the lessons to liturgical acts and/or homiletical options for the day on which they occur. How the texts have been used in the Christian tradition will sometimes be illustrated to stimulate the thinking of preachers and planners of worship services.

I. OLD TESTAMENT TEXTS

A. The Old Testament Lesson

1. Setting

2. Structure

3. Significance

B. Psalm

1. Setting

2. Structure

3. Significance

II. NEW TESTAMENT TEXTS

A. The Epistle

1. Setting

2. Structure

3. Significance

B. The Gospel

1. Setting

2. Structure

3. Significance

Why We Use the Lectionary

Although many denominations have been officially or unofficially using some form of the lectionary for many years, some pastors are still unclear about where it comes from, why some lectionaries differ from denomination to denomination, and why the use of a lectionary is to be preferred to a more random sampling of scripture.

Simply put, the use of a lectionary provides a more diverse scriptural diet for God's people, and it can help protect the congregation from the whims and prejudices of the pastor and other worship planners. Faithful use of the lectionary means that preachers must deal with texts they had rather ignore, but about which the congregation may have great concern and interest. An apocalyptic text, such as we encounter in this volume on the First Sunday of Advent, might be a case in point. Adherence to the lectionary can be an antidote to that homiletical arrogance that says, "I know what my people need," and in humility acknowledges that the Word of God found in scripture may speak to more needs on Sunday morning than we even know exist, when we seek to proclaim faithfully the message we have wrestled from the text.

The lectionary may also serve as a resource for liturgical content. The psalm is intended to be a response to the Old Testament lesson, and not read as a lesson itself, but beyond that the lessons may inform the content of prayers of confession, intercession, and petition. Some lessons may be adapted as affirmations of faith, as in *The United Methodist Hymnal,* nos. 887-889; the United Church of Christ's *Hymnal,* nos. 429-30; and the Presbyterian *Worshipbook,* no. 30. The "Celebration" entries for each day will call attention to these opportunities from time to time.

Pastors and preachers in the free-church tradition should think of the lectionary as a primary resource for preaching and worship, but need to remember that the lectionary was made for them and not they for the lectionary. The lectionary may serve as the inspiration for a separate series of lessons and sermons that will include texts not in the present edition, or having chosen one of the lectionary passages as the basis for the day's sermon, the preacher may wish to make an independent choice of the other lessons to supplement and illustrate the primary text. The lectionary will be of most value when its use is not a cause for legalism but for inspiration. Pastors who experience a love/hate relationship with the lectionary will gain much sympathy and guidance from Eugene Lowry's penetrating analysis in *Living with the Lectionary: Preaching Through the Revised Common Lectionary* (Nashville: Abingdon Press, 1992).

Just as there are no perfect preachers, there are no perfect lectionaries. The Revised Common Lectionary, upon which this series is based, is the result of the work of many years by the Consultation on Common Texts and is a response to ongoing evaluation of the Common Lectionary (1983) by pastors and scholars from the several participating denominations. The current interest in the lectionary can be traced back to the Second Vatican Council, which ordered lectionary revision for the Roman Catholic Church:

> The treasures of the Bible are to be opened up more lavishly, so that richer fare may be provided for the faithful at the table of God's Word. In this way a more representative portion of the holy Scriptures will be read to the people over a set cycle of years. (Walter Abbott, ed., *The Documents of Vatican II* [Piscataway, N.J.: New Century, 1974], p. 155)

The example thus set by Roman Catholics inspired Protestants to take more seriously the place of the Bible in their services and sermons, and soon many denominations had issued their own three-year cycles, based generally on the Roman Catholic model but with their own modifications. This explains why some discrepancies and variations appear in different forms of the lectionary. The Revised Common Lectionary (RCL) is an effort to increase agreement among the churches. A table at the end of the volume will list the differences between the RCL and the Roman Catholic, Episcopal, and Lutheran lectionaries. Where no entry is made, all are in agreement with the RCL.

For those unacquainted with the general pattern of the lectionary, a brief word of explanation may be helpful for sermon preparation.

(1) The three years are each distinguished by one of the Synoptic Gospels: Matthew in A, Mark in B, Luke in C. John is distributed over the three years with a heavy emphasis during Lent and Easter. (2) Two types of readings are used. During the periods of Advent to Epiphany and Lent to Pentecost, the readings are usually topical, that is, there is some common theme among them. During the Sundays after Epiphany and Pentecost the readings are continuous, with no necessary connection between the lessons. In the period covered by this volume (Advent, Christmas, Epiphany), there is a thematic connection between the Old Testament lesson and the Gospel during the Sundays after Epiphany, but the epistle lesson begins a continuous reading from I Corinthians. The preacher begins, then, with at least four preaching options: to deal with either one of the lessons on their own or to work with the dialogue between the Old Testament lesson and the Gospel. Perhaps it should also be added that though the psalm is intended to be a response by the people to the Old Testament lesson—rather than as a lesson on its own—this in no way suggests that it cannot be used as the text for the sermon.

This is the first of four volumes that will deal with the lessons for the entire C Cycle of the Christian year. The second volume will include Ash Wednesday through the Day of Pentecost. The third volume begins with Trinity Sunday (the First Sunday After Pentecost) and includes all the lessons for June, July, and August. The fourth volume finishes the remainder of the year, including the lessons for All Saints' Day (November 1). Years A and B have been published previously, also in two series of four volumes each.

A note on language: We have used the term *Old Testament* in this series because that is the language employed by the Consultation on Common Texts, at least up to this point. Pastors and worship committees may wish to consider alternative terms such as *First Testament* or *Hebrew Scriptures* that do not imply that those writings somehow have less value than the rest of the Christian Bible. Another option is to refer to *First Lesson* (always from the Hebrew Scriptures), *Second Lesson* (from Acts, Revelation, or the epistles), and *Gospel.*

THE PASCHAL MYSTERY
AND ADVENT

Preachers and liturgical planners who seek to take seriously the Christian year as the basis of their work need to remember first of all that the purpose for the year is to allow us to focus on particular aspects of the Easter proclamation and their relevance to Christian life and thought. Easter is at the center of the Christian faith; without Easter there could be no Christian faith, only the Good Friday memory of a man who tried valiantly to make a witness about God and failed. The Christian year grew out of the Church's desire to participate as fully as possible in every aspect of the Paschal mystery by dynamically remembering and thus sharing in the salvation-giving events recorded in scripture.

Thus understood, the observance of the Christian year is not the same as the annual cyclical celebrations of the Greco-Roman mystery religions. In the mystery religions, the gods needed to have the ritual activities performed in order to assist them in bringing about the salvation of the performers; the gods were dependent upon the worshipers for their very existence. It was the activity of the faithful that brought the god back to life. In Christian worship, we acknowledge what God has done and is doing by virtue of God's own will and power. So for Christians, the Resurrection is a fact proclaimed and experienced, rather than a need of God that the worshiper is called upon to help bring about. God is responsible for the Easter triumph, not us or even our faith in the Resurrection.

This means that the Church does not approach Advent pretending that Jesus has not yet been born or that we know nothing about Calvary and the empty tomb. Advent is celebrated in the light of the Christ-event; it is an examination and celebration of the Easter mystery from this side of the empty tomb. We do not sing Christmas carols or preach sermon series on "They Met at the Manger" during Advent because we are ignorant of Christmas, but because we wish to experience and proclaim that hope which in Israel waited in faith for the Messiah during the darkest and most desolate of times, and which since Easter still waits "for the revealing of our Lord Jesus Christ" (I Cor. 1:7, Second Reading, First Sunday of Advent, Year B).

Advent is the Janus of the Christian year. It looks backward at Israel's expectation of a Messiah (the Old Testament lessons), and it looks forward to the consummation, to the ultimate triumph of Christ over the power of sin and death that was begun on that first Easter Day. Advent, in its message of judgment and the reign of Christ, is as much a result of Easter as it is an anticipation of Easter and may be considered the end of the Christian year as appropriately as it is considered the beginning. Because we mortals are linear beings, creatures of time, we usually want things to have a beginning and an end. Because Advent does deal with the expectation of the Messiah and the preparations for his birth, there is a logic in using it to begin the annual cycle.

Once again, we must remember that this is not a cyclic event as in the mystery religions, where the god is dependent upon our actions for his or her existence and where the same event occurs over and over again. We may use the term *cycle* as a matter of convenience, but the fact is that we are not the same persons who celebrated Advent last year, and we are not the same persons who will celebrate Advent next year. Yearly we bring another 365 days of grace to our celebration, and so our insight into the Paschal mystery is deeper and our observance conditioned by the previous year's "dangers, toils, and fears." We are not the same people doing the same thing year after year. The hope we bring to this year's Advent is not the same hope we brought last year, for it has been tempered and informed by "the encouragement of the scriptures" (Romans 15:4, Second Reading, Second Sunday of Advent, Year A), as during the year we have sought to "put on the Lord Jesus Christ" (Romans 13:14, First Sunday of Advent, Year A), so that we "may be blameless at his coming" (I Thessalonians 3:13, First Sunday of Advent, Year C).

The Advent Gospels in Year C: An Overview

Before looking at the individual Sundays and their lessons, it is important to notice the sequence of the Gospel readings, since they tend to dictate the choice of the other readings and the primary theme for each day. This quick overview should also make clearer the progression of the Sundays as well as the internal structure of the season.

On the First Sunday, the Gospel reading is Luke's narrative of the prophecy of the coming of the Son of Man. We begin the year with a consideration of the end of all things, of the triumph of the One at the end of time who began his victory when he overcame death on Easter Day. In some ways this is as much an end to the year as it is a beginning, because two weeks earlier the Gospel lesson will have been from the Markan apocalypse (Mark 13:1-8), and last week the Gospel reading recounted Jesus' declaration to Pilate that "my kingdom is not from this world" (John 18:33-37). We begin the story at the end. The following fifty-one Sundays might be viewed as a kind of flashback until we work our way back to the end again with the announcement on the Last Sunday After Pentecost (Christ the King) that we have been transferred "into the kingdom of [God's] beloved Son" (Colossians 1:13).

On the Second Sunday, we are introduced to John the Baptist, that rugged figure who stands with a foot in each Testament, and on this Sunday we see and hear him preaching a message of repentance in the tradition of Amos, who is being read in Year Two of the Daily Office Lectionary during this time. (The Daily Office Lectionary may be found in the *Book of Common Prayer,* pp. 933-1001; the *Lutheran Book of Worship,* pp. 179-92; and the Presbyterian *Supplemental Liturgical Resource 5,* Daily Prayer, pp. 395-419).

On the Third Sunday, the Testaments merge in the preaching of John who denies that he is the Christ, and who testifies to the greater One who is coming. We have moved, as it were, into the New Testament from the Old by means of this bridge character.

On the Fourth Sunday, with the stage having been earlier set by John, we do a flashback within the flashback, and we see Mary going to visit John's mother, where John even in the womb testifies to the presence of the greater One and Mary rejoices over God's regard for her. Only now are we ready for the trip to Bethlehem and the manger.

The Liturgical Environment

Colors. Purple has been the customary color for Advent in the Western Church since the sixteenth century. There has been a recent trend to the use of blue, based on the inventories of some medieval churches. Rigidity over the use of color did not come about until the Reformation, when the invention of printing allowed everything to be rubricized and regulated. The catalogs of publishing houses notwithstanding, purple is not primarily a color of penitence; that is a symbolism attached to the color after the fact, once purple had been assigned to Lent and then to Advent. The penitential character of Lent gave symbolic interpretation to the color. In the ancient world, purple was the color of royalty, since only a royal income could afford the dye that made it possible. Purple, then, points to the kingship of Christ, "the Lord's anointed, great David's greater Son." We decorate our churches in purple or royal blue (not a pastel blue) to prepare for the coming of the king.

The use of a pink candle in the Advent wreath is an imitation of a Roman Catholic practice that is not even required of churches outside the city of Rome itself. The observance of Lent/Easter is older than that of Advent/Christmas, and so the liturgical practices of Advent tended to be modeled on those that had developed earlier for Lent. An idiosyncrasy in the Roman practice developed because by the early Middle Ages the custom had developed for the pope, as a sign of special favor, to give a golden rose to persons he especially esteemed. He did this on the Fourth Sunday in Lent, and in honor of the occasion the churches were decorated with rose-colored paraments. The day came to be seen as a respite before plunging into the rigors of the last days of the Lenten fast. It also helped that the first word of the introit for that Sunday was "laetare," rejoice. Because Advent was looked upon as a "little Lent," it became the custom on the third Sunday (when the first word of the introit was "gaudete," also "rejoice") to use rose vestments to parallel the Lenten pattern.

Advent wreaths. Advent wreaths have become popular visual aids in many churches to mark the time through Advent, and the making of them provides activities for the church school, family nights, and similar meetings. Often the products are then used as a part of individual or family devotions throughout the season. Family units are often employed to do the lighting of the wreath at the beginning of the church service each Sunday. (Pastors might want to examine what kind of silent judgment this pronounces against single persons. Is it a reinforcement of the popular myth that "Christmas is only for children" or that the season can only be appreciated in a family context?) Please note that the various candles on the Advent wreath don't mean anything! To paraphrase Archibald MacLeish's comment on poetry, "An Advent wreath should not mean, but be." Symbolization, the attribution of one meaning to a thing that does not in itself evoke that meaning, is a frequent liturgical error; we inhibit or restrict meaning by insisting that things should mean only the one thing we arbitrarily assign to them. If individuals or groups are going to prepare their own liturgies for the lighting of the wreath, and insist on attributing meaning to each candle, then the meaning (or more accurately, the theme) should grow out of a consideration of the lessons for the day, and that theme may appropriately change from year to year.

Chrismons. A more recent appearance has been made in many churches by chrismon trees hung with symbols of Christ. It is difficult to avoid the suspicion that these are a means of sneaking Christmas trees onto the scene early. If they are to be used at all, they certainly should not be evergreens. It would be preferable to use something of bare branches only. Following the same logic, the hanging of the greens is inappropriate before the Fourth Sunday of Advent, no matter how close to Christmas itself that may be. The absence of any altar flowers during these four Sundays can be a remarkable contrast to the explosion of poinsettias that is to come.

Silence. Advent is a time to encourage the use of silence. Waiting and watching are major themes of the season, and they can be reinforced by ritual silence that should stand in marked contrast to the musical merriment of the Christmas celebration. Roman Catholic, Lutheran, and Anglican churches have customarily suppressed the use of the *Gloria in excelsis Deo* ("Glory be to God on high") during Advent, so that this song of the angels is heard with a fresh appreciation at the first service of Christmas. An absence of organ voluntaries may also be appropriate.

A hymn. The hymn, "O Come, O Come, Emmanuel," and the "O" antiphons on which it is based, provide a number of significant images for use as Advent visuals on bulletins, paraments, vestments, and so

17

on. (Different versions include no. 211 in *The United Methodist Hymnal;* no. 56 in the Episcopal *The Hymnal,* 1982, and pages 174-75 in *The Lutheran Book of Worship*.) Among them are a crown and scepter for the expected king, a key, a star of David, a Jesse tree, and a rising sun. The application of the title "Wisdom" (Sophia or Sapientia) to Christ in the text of "O Come, O Come, Emmanuel" reminds us of the sexual inclusiveness of redemption since Wisdom has often been portrayed as a female. This use is also found in the hymn "O Word of God Incarnate." The thoughtful pastor might wish to relate these images to the New Testament lesson for the Second Sunday of Advent in Year A with its reference to the scriptures. It was because this lesson was the standard one in the old lectionary that for many years the second Sunday in December (frequently the second of Advent) was celebrated as Bible Sunday. Cranmer's collect, "Blessed Lord, who hast caused all holy scriptures to be written for our learning," was composed for the Second Sunday of Advent. Bible Sunday is now officially the Sunday before Thanksgiving Day, which doesn't give it any better chance of recognition than it had before, so this Sunday in Year A might still serve as a time to emphasize in some way the scriptures as the cradle that holds the Incarnate Word, as the pulpit through which the apostles continue to proclaim what they saw and heard. Christ as Wisdom extends beyond the image of the Bible alone, and worship planners are challenged to think of other visual and symbolic expressions that may be employed.

Because "O Come, O Come, Emmanuel" is so rich with images, its use ought not be restricted to once during the season (particularly now that many hymnals include seven rather than four stanzas). The stanzas might be divided among the Sundays and used as a part of the lighting of the Advent wreath or some other act of worship. This would allow a familiar Advent hymn to be used each Sunday and would permit more time to explore one or two Advent images more fully. The stanzas of the hymn could be sung in response to the recitation of the complementary "O" antiphons. Stanza 1 alone would be used on the First Sunday of Advent, 2 and 3 on the Second Sunday, 4 and 5 on the Third Sunday, and 6 and 7 on the Fourth Sunday. An appropriate collect could conclude the rite, particularly if the lighting of the wreath is also the opening act of worship.

First Sunday of Advent

Old Testament Texts

Jeremiah 33:14-16 is a divine proclamation about a future restoration, while Psalm 25:1-10 is a lament over present evil.

The Lesson: *Jeremiah 33:14-16*

A Future Salvation

Setting. Jeremiah prophesied in Jerusalem at the end of the monarchical period and through the fall of the kingdom of Judah, when Judah was conquered by the Babylonians in 587 B.C.E. The final years of the kingdom of Judah were chaotic times because the whole world was at war. The Assyrians, who had ruled the ancient Near East for nearly two centuries, were overthrown by the Babylonians in 612 B.C.E., and the effects of such a huge reshuffling of world power were not yet clear to smaller nations like Judah. Should they declare independence from all the superpowers? Should they align themselves with the Babylonians? Would the Assyrians reemerge? And what about the ever-present Egyptians? All of these political concerns were also intimately interwoven and partially in conflict with Israel's sense of being the elect people of God, which for them meant that their nation existed not by political alliance at all but by divine promise and that its existence was guaranteed by God. Thus the calm at the center of the political storm was Israel's belief that they were ultimately secure because their nation was protected by God.

Much of the prophetic ministry of Jeremiah was an attack on the one point where the king and leaders of Judah seemed to agree, namely that their national future was secure because of their election (see the Temple sermon in chapter 7). Jeremiah criticized this mixing of God and country by becoming a prophet of judgment and doom. This focus is underscored in Jeremiah's call when God informs him that he would be an instrument "to pluck up and to pull down, to destroy and overthrow" nations and vast kingdoms (Jeremiah 1:10). The result of Jeremiah's call is that while the leaders of Israel approached the chaotic political situation with hope in order to see what alliance might ensure their present existence as a nation, Jeremiah evaluated the same situation as being hopeless because he believed that God was intent on destroying Judah for its misunderstanding of salvation. Judean leaders were convinced that salvation meant political security.

Jeremiah 32–33 illustrates Jeremiah's prophetic ministry of judgment. In 32:1-6 we are told that Jerusalem is under siege by the Babylonians, a siege so thorough that in 33:10-13 we learn the countryside is reduced to a wasteland. Even though the king and the leaders of Judah hang on to a present hope that somehow they may survive the Babylonian onslaught, Jeremiah sees the situation differently and states the unthinkable that the Babylonian siege of Jerusalem will actually succeed because it is the judgment of God against Judah. King Zedekiah is shocked by such heresy and throws Jeremiah in jail, because even the smallest child in Jerusalem knows that God dwelt in the Temple and certainly would not allow the Babylonians to take over the city of God.

King Zedekiah is wrong. The hope of salvation cannot be anchored so firmly in the present existence of the nation. Yet just when Jeremiah's message of doom is being confirmed with Jerusalem on the verge of being sacked, God speaks a new word of future hope, which is our lesson for this First Sunday of Advent. This text is unexpected, for in the midst of the besieged wasteland, God paints a utopian vision of the land in 33:14-16.

Structure. The use of "day" in prophetic speeches (see vv. 14, 15, 16a) usually signals eschatological prophecies, which are visions of a future time. This clue provides insight into why 33:14-16 contrasts so sharply to its larger context in Jeremiah 32–33. The prophet has left the present situation of the Babylonian siege behind. A variety of shifts accompanies the change of focus from present to future. Verse 14 shifts our attention in three ways: first, temporally, from the present to an indefinite future; second, from divine judgment to salvation; and third, from the present wasteland of war to a future utopia. Verse 15 explains why there can be a future hope. It is because God has promised to David that one of his seed would rule the land in justice and righteousness. Verse 16 shifts the focus from God's action in bringing about a future salvation to a description of what it will be like for the people of God to live in this renewed land. Here we learn that in contrast to the present peril, the new Jerusalem will be a place of security. Finally, v. 16b underscores how this future security is rooted in God alone. This point is made when we are told that those who experience this future salvation will automatically credit it to God by proclaiming, "The Lord is our righteousness."

Significance. The structure underscores how 33:14-16 is eschatological, which makes this text appropriate for Advent. In addition, the motif of the Davidic promise lends itself to a christological interpretation. These two foci lead to the conclusion that Jesus is the fulfillment of the promise to David, who ushers in God's salvation. This conclusion, however, is too easy and does not lend itself to preaching, because it tends to isolate the passage from its larger context in Jeremiah 32–33, where we have seen that it has an unexpected and surprising function of promise in the midst of chaos. A better avenue for preaching is to probe the text in its present narrative context in order to provide insight into two essential components of Advent: that security cannot be in present political structures for the people of God and that the fulfillment of salvation will be unexpected because it is in God's hands alone.

The problem of security. As we noted earlier, Jeremiah's word of judgment to Judah was in reaction to their misunderstanding of hope. The king and leaders of Judah thought that their hope rested in their continued existence as a nation. Although their motives were pious, this mixing of God and country blinded them to a larger vision of God's future salvation. Because of this blindness Jeremiah was called to be a prophet of destruction.

The unexpected character of salvation. At the point when things look their worst, with the prophet in jail and Jerusalem in the final days of the bloody siege, God directs Jeremiah in 32:6-25 to buy his uncle's land at Anathoth, even though the Babylonians already controlled that city. This instruction would be as appealing as a modern directive to buy the Love Canal, which is the name of property that has been infected by toxic waste. One would prefer at least a few market indicators of why good money should be thrown after bad. The only economic analysis that Jeremiah receives is the rhetorical question from God, "Is anything too hard for me?" The implied answer is, of course, "No," and here is the point of contact with Advent. That God is able to perform the unexpected makes Advent possible, but it does not go to the heart of Advent. Advent goes beyond the simple celebration of divine power and gives that power a forward direction. God is committed to a new world. Our dual belief that nothing is too hard for God and that God's promised salvation must reach its fulfillment gives rise to the utopian vision in 33:14-16 which informs our Advent faith.

The Response: *Psalm 25:1-10*

Waiting in Hope

Setting. Psalm 25 explores another aspect of Advent that has not been part of our discussion of Jeremiah 33:14-16, the experience of waiting in hope for the fulfillment of salvation. In many respects Psalm 25 presupposes a text like Jeremiah 33:14-16, because it is a psalm of lament. We can only lament if we have experienced the salvation of God and seen the vision of salvation as it is described in Jeremiah 33:14-16, while also knowing that the present moment is removed from both. This is the situation of the psalmist in Psalm 25, who is experiencing a gap between a vision of what salvation should be and present life.

Structure. Psalm 25 has a difficult structure. One problem is the acrostic framework, in which every line begins with a letter of the Hebrew alphabet. Another problem is the limitation of this psalm to vv. 1-10 in the lectionary. If only vv. 1-10 are read, then the psalm must be separated between petition (vv. 1-7) and praise (vv. 8-10).

For better worship, a reading of the entire psalm yields a three-part structure of petition (vv. 1-7), confession about the faithfulness of God (vv. 8-14), and a concluding series of petitions (vv. 15-22), now strengthened because of the psalmist's confessions about God in the previous section. The three-part structure of lament-confidence-lament probes more deeply the nature of Christian lamentation during Advent. We do not simply petition God and reach confident conclusions, as the boundaries of the lectionary would suggest. Often lamenting and waiting in hope can be an extended state-of-being, as the larger structure of the psalm would suggest.

Significance. Verse 2 sets the tone for the petitions in the first section (vv. 1-7), when the psalmist begins with the affirmation, "To you, O Lord, I lift up my soul. / O my God, in you I trust." The trust of the psalmist is a quality of faith that affirms the reality of God's salvation even though the experience of it is presently remote. The second section in vv. 8-14 provides the reason for the psalmist's trust through a series of affirmations about the character of God. God is good, leads, teaches, pardons, brings promises to fulfillment, and is a friend to those who fear him. Verses 15-22 return to petitions, which now build on the confessions about God. The movement of lament-confession-lament provides a perspective on how we wait in hope. Psalm 25 explores our need to live a life of faith in tension with our present world, which may force us to lament and to wait in hope as a state of being. In our daily human experience with pestilence and conflict, despite the relentless cycle of the Christian year, we know that Advent doesn't always lead directly to Christmas.

New Testament Texts

The readings for this first Sunday in Year C bring together striking passages from Paul's epistle and the gospel according to Luke. Both texts have a prominent future dimension in that they mention the coming of the Lord Jesus (I Thessalonians) or the Son of Man (Luke). In both passages the expected future coming is of great significance because the coming and the Coming One lay claims on a present that determines the course of current human life, especially in terms of Christian community living.

The Epistle: *1 Thessalonians 3:9-13*

Gratitude and Service Before the Coming of the Lord

Setting. First Thessalonians is thought to be the earliest letter from Paul that was preserved by the later Church. As such, it is probably the first piece of Christian literature that is available to the subsequent Church. In this letter, the apostle writes from Corinth to advise the Thessalonian congregation about matters of importance in their thought and life. In brief, the Christians in Thessalonica have experienced persecution by others who are nonbelievers. The precise nature of the difficulties that the Thessalonians experienced is not clear, but Paul writes to these believers to confirm and to direct them in their life as a Christian community. More precisely, in chapter three of this letter Paul explains why he wrote to the Thessalonians. He explains that he desires to visit them, but he cannot; so, he writes this letter.

Structure. As Paul expresses his desire to see the Thessalonians, his thought proceeds in three movements, as is recognized by the paragraphing of critical editions of the Greek text and in translations such as the NRSV (3:1-5, 6-10, 11-13). In this week's reading, vv. 9-10 are the final portion of Paul's second round of statements, reporting his gratitude and concern for the Thessalonians; then, vv. 11-13 pronounce a profound benediction on the recipients of the letter. Gratitude, concern, and blessing are the major themes suggested by this passage for proclamation.

Significance. Paul's mood is one of yearning, even of expectation, as he tells the members of the Thessalonian congregation that he wants to be with them, that he expects to be with them, but that at present he cannot be there. From this mood the apostle turns to express his thankfulness to God for the joy he enjoys because of the faith of the Thessalonians. This joy, however, is not merely a fantastic feeling of well-being, as is evident from Paul's report of his prayerful concern to return to the Thessalonians and to work among them for the development of their faith. Away from this congregation and unable at the time to be with them—in yearning, thankfulness, and prayer—Paul petitions God and the Lord Jesus to direct him to the Thessalonians and to realize in abundance a kind of life for this congregation that will be acceptable to God, as God through Jesus moves in judgment over the course of human affairs.

The mood of expectation and yearning expressed as thankfulness and prayerful concern make this text appropriate for the Advent season. Above all, the mention of the coming of the Lord Jesus in v. 13 suggests the use of this passage at this time of year. Several specific items in Paul's remarks bear reflection. First, in the arena of Christian relations, Paul demonstrates the appropriateness of genuine gratitude to God for the experience of Christian community. Yet such gratitude is not merely passive but active. Paul's gratitude leads to the prayerful desire to be of even more benefit to the Thessalonian church, so one sees gratitude to God and service to the church linked hand in hand.

Second, in the benediction Paul pronounces on the Thessalonian Christians, one observes the apostle's clear recognition of God's guidance in the developments of the life of the church. The effect of God's direction in the growth and development of the church is specific and even more qualitative than quantitative, for Paul expects God's blessings to result in the mutual devotion of the members of the congregation to one another so that the whole community of faith is built up or edified.

Third, in the final portion of the benediction (v. 13) Paul clearly anticipates that God will move to evaluate the conditions of Christian life. He states this in terms of the expectation of the coming of the Lord Jesus. In other words, God's future sets the standards for the present. Moreover, in the person of the Coming One, the Lord Jesus, God makes known God's self and the way of life to which God calls and directs us.

The Gospel: *Luke 21:25-36*

"When You See . . . You Know"

Setting. The readers of Luke's story of the ministry of Jesus have traveled a long distance by the time they encounter this reading in the twenty-first chapter of the Gospel. Luke's particular point of view regarding Jesus clearly affects the shape and style of his presentation of the message of salvation. Luke's own favorite designation for Jesus is "the Lord," and this high regard for Jesus is matched in the presentation by Luke's beautiful style and special narrative touches.

Careful study of this week's Gospel reading in comparison with the parallel passages in Mark 13 and Matthew 24 helps locate some of Luke's special touches (more on this below). In general, however, in approaching this passage one should be aware that the major portion of Luke 21 is a collection of prophetic messages spoken by Jesus, and presented here in the final days of his ministry when he came to Jerusalem shortly before Passover.

Structure. The verses of the lesson form three distinguishable sections of material. (1) Verses 25-28 are a prophecy concerning the coming of the Son of Man, which is cast in the highly dramatic, even symbolic, language of apocalyptic literature. (2) The second unit (vv. 29-33) is actually a cluster of teachings and sayings, perhaps originally spoken independently, brought together here to form a multifaceted prophetic lesson. Finally, (3) vv. 34-36 are a coherent statement issuing complementary words of warning and admonition. An ambitious preacher may deal with this entire lesson in one sermon, but either of the sections can be dealt with alone without undermining the integrity of the text. Yet, given the season, one will find that the language concerning "coming" in the first and third sections assists one in moving more rapidly to the theme of expectation than the less direct vocabulary concerning the drawing near of the kingdom of God.

Significance. The first section (vv. 25-28) with its apocalyptic language, images, and thought presents a challenge to the preachers of today. It is helpful to recognize that the language was generated from a strong sense of dissatisfaction with the author's present reality and an equally strong yearning for an altered future—both of which spring from an absolute conviction that God ultimately exercises authority over all creation, including the course of history. The language of apocalyptic conviction is cosmic in its dimensions—thus, the talk about the sun, the moon, and the other fixtures of the universe. The goal of this manner of thinking and speaking is to produce awe in the hearer, so that the conviction that God is indeed in control of the world (perhaps despite appearances!) comes home to the one listening to or reading such texts. What is most striking in this passage is the movement from the awe-inspiring words about the distress of the universe, the feeble reaction of humanity, and the majestic coming of the Son of Man in vv. 25-27 to the encouraging exhortation in v. 28. The cosmic distress is but evidence of the power of God that is at work to bring about the redemption of those who believe in and recognize the authoritative work of God.

The cluster of statements which follows in vv. 29-33 is in one way more self-evident and in another more enigmatic. The parable of the fig tree is a picture lesson: "When you see these things . . . you know that. . . ." From this simple argument, by analogy, v. 31 delivers a lesson. When "these things" (presumably the signs of cosmic distress in vv. 25-27) take place, the Christian community (all the "you's" here are plural in Greek) can be assured that God's full control over a rebellious creation is being finally established. The statement that "the Kingdom of God is near" alludes to the active coming of the Kingdom—that is, God moves toward creation and humanity. We are not simply left to find God or even commanded to do what is necessary to be in God's presence; God is portrayed here as moving toward us in a manner and speed that are of God's own determining. The promises of vv. 32-33 underscore the veracity and dependability of Jesus' teaching. Verse 32 is particularly problematic, but if one gives Luke credit for being sane, this statement may indicate that he and other early Christians understood the promise of redemption and the coming of the Kingdom in relation to the distress at Christ's crucifixion, rather than in relation to some as of yet unrealized occurrence.

Finally, vv. 34-36 issue a fairly gentle warning. Those who follow Jesus are told to beware of having divided attention (one thinks naturally of Søren Kierkegaard's purity of heart), of squandering their time in ill-use, and of devoting themselves to matters of less than ultimate (from God's point of view) importance. To underline this warning, we read of the promise of real, final judgment. In the face of this awesome reality, v. 36 admonishes us to attentiveness to God's leadership and prayerfulness in relationship to our human condition. The final word in the lesson about standing before the Son of Man is both threat and assurance. We will be judged, but by the very one who we believe died for our redemption. Sermons should seek to arouse a sense of the necessity to live according to God's standards, without lapsing into mere moralism.

Advent 1: The Celebration

The theme of judgment that is presented by today's lessons provides an occasion for recalling the traditional meditation upon the "four last things:" death, judgment, heaven, and hell. These can provide a sobering antidote to the festive mood that is already beginning to besot the secular mind, which far too often tells the Church how to order its celebrative life rather than the other way around.

This meditation may appropriately come as part of the penitential rite, which should characterize the beginning of worship during Advent. It may on this Sunday even precede the opening organ voluntary as a kind of introduction to the season itself.

THE GREETING

Grace and peace to you from the One who was and who is and who is to come.
Behold, he comes with clouds, and every eye shall see him.

INTRODUCTION TO ADVENT AND CALL TO PENITENCE

In Advent we look forward. We rekindle the eager hope and fear with which the Old Testament prophets looked forward to the coming of the promised Messiah; we prepare ourselves to celebrate his birth at Christmas.

When the Lord Christ came to live among us, he taught us to look forward to the hour when we shall each be called from this world through death: the crowning point of every life, when we appear before him for judgment.

He taught us also, and above all, to see our lives in his divine perspective, to long for the day when he will come again, the point beyond which all looking forward will cease, for time will have come to an end. Then all will be united and perfected in heaven, save what has been lost to hell.

Today let us meditate on these four last things: death, judgment, heaven, and hell. Let us examine our preparation for death and eternal life, in order that we may be strengthened in hope, moved to thank God for divine grace, and inspired to deeper penitence and greater love. [adapted from *The Promise of His Glory* (London: Church House Publishing, 1991), p. 103]

AN ACT OF PENITENCE

In the midst of life we are in death;
from whom can we seek help?
From you alone, O Lord,
who by our sins are justly angered.

Holy God, Holy and Mighty,
Holy and merciful Savior,
deliver us not into the bitterness of eternal death.

Lord, you know the secrets of our hearts:
shut not your ears to our prayers,
but spare us, O Lord.

Holy God, Holy and Mighty,
Holy and merciful Savior,
deliver us not into the bitterness of eternal death.

O worthy and eternal Judge,
do not let the pains of death
turn us away from you at our last hour.

Holy God, Holy and Mighty,
Holy and merciful Savior,
deliver us not into the bitterness of eternal death.

[silent recollection]

Deliver us, Lord, from every evil,
and grant us peace in our day.
In your mercy keep us free from sin
and protect us from all anxiety
as we wait in joyful hope
for the coming of our Savior Jesus Christ. Amen.

SUNG PETITION

(tune: Hamburg or Rockingham)
O, on that day, that wrathful day,
When all to judgment wake from clay,
Be thou, O Christ, the sinner's stay,
Though heaven and earth shall pass away.
(Sir Walter Scott)

29

WORDS OF ASSURANCE
In the tender compassion of our God
the dawn from on high shall break upon us,
to shine on those who dwell in darkness
and the shadow of death,
and to guide our feet into the way of peace.
In the name of Jesus Christ, you are forgiven.
In the name of Jesus Christ, you are forgiven. **Amen.**

The above penitential order may be used next Sunday as well, but it is not appropriate on the Sundays following since those lessons are moving into the theme of the Annunciation and away from that of judgment. Although the tone of this order seems severe, it provides a vivid connection to the Paschal mystery (see the introduction), because it makes clear how the Incarnation is God's response to humankind's sinful condition.

Second Sunday of Advent

Old Testament Texts

Malachi 3:1-4 is part of a disputation between the prophet and the priests about whether God is just and reliable. Luke 1:68-79 is the Benedictus of Zechariah, which he sang when his son, John, was circumcised.

The Lesson: *Malachi 3:1-4*

Where Is God's Justice?

Setting. Scholars are divided over the exact time and circumstances of the literary formation of the book of Malachi and how it came to stand as an independent book. The title or superscription to the book begins by referring to an "oracle." This word is also used in Zechariah 9:1 and 12:1, which has led scholars to explore the relationship between these sections of Zechariah and the book of Malachi. The question is raised as to whether the headings signal three separate collections of sayings, of which two were attached to Zechariah, while the third was made to form an independent book. Such a theory of the formation of the book raises the question of whether Malachi is really the name of a prophet or simply a title meaning "my messenger." A decision on this issue will probably not effect how the text is preached, and thus the reader is encouraged to explore these problems of literary formation and authorship in more detail in other commentaries. The time of the oracles, however, are important for preaching the text. Malachi addresses some of the issues that arise in Nehemiah (tithing, divorce, and mixed marriage). These similarities suggest that Malachi is post-exilic. Furthermore, references to the Temple in 1:10 and 3:1 suggest that it has already been rebuilt. These are important clues for preaching, for they suggest that Malachi was probably written after the big events of the return from exile and the rebuilding of the Temple, at a time when those who had returned from Babylon were settling down into a routine after these radical events. Read Second Isaiah and Haggai where the return from exile and the construction of the Temple were interpreted in cosmological scope, and where the writers were confident of seeing the hand of God moving all of history so that Israel and Jerusalem could be the center of world events, which is promised as a new salvation. The oracles of Malachi are written in the wake of these larger-than-life events, when the rebuilt Jerusalem with its Temple was beginning to look more like a backwater town than the cosmic center of the universe, where nations were destined to meet. The setting of Malachi, therefore, would appear to be one in which daily routine now threatens to extinguish cosmological visions of salvation. This is the point of departure for preaching Malachi. The danger to faith that is being explored in this book is indifference and cynicism to the presence of God in the daily routines of the people of God.

Structure. Most scholars would agree that the boundaries of the lectionary text must be expanded when preaching from 3:1-4 to embrace the wider 2:17–3:5. The structure of the larger unit divides into two parts: 2:17 presents a disputation between the prophet and most likely Levitical priests, 3:1-5 is a divine response to the issues raised in 2:17.

Significance. Apathy and indifference is a problem throughout the book of Malachi. The prophet states the problem in the opening chapter with regard to sacrifices. Although the choicest offerings are vowed as a gift to God, they rarely found their way to the altar. Somehow in the bureaucratic shuffle, God got the seconds, or the remaindered merchandise. The prophet states that the routine of sacrifice and worship in the absence of larger salvific events has led to a cynicism in Israel that now wearies God (1:13). The issue is taken a step further in the Old Testament lesson for this Sunday. A disputation is set forward in 2:17 through quotations that are shaped into a question-and-answer format. The prophet states, "You have wearied the Lord with your words." Then the prophet quotes his opponents' reply, "How have we wearied him?" Quotation continues when the prophet uses the words of his opponents to document their cynicism concerning divine justice, "By saying, 'All who do evil are good in the sight of the Lord, and he delights in them.' Or by asking, 'Where is the God of justice?' " The attitude of the prophet's opponents is a cynical pragmatism. Good is evil and evil is good; what matters are the results in the ongoing daily routine of life.

Malachi 3:1-5 is God's answer to the question about justice. The eschatological discourse about a future messenger, therefore, should not be interpreted so much as a comforting word as much as a challenge to the community of faith that finds itself lost in daily routine and vulnerable to a pragmatic cynicism. The message of these verses is two-sided in answering the question of where divine justice is to be found. On the one hand, the prophet states that further larger-than-life events will indeed happen in the context of the people of God. In particular, the prophet states that further acts of divine justice will purify the people of God, and this is a word of hope (vv. 2-4). On the other hand, those who had become cynical and pragmatic concerning divine justice will be shaken from their stupor when they are confronted by divine justice in the form of judgment rather than salvation (v. 5).

Malachi 2:17–3:5 is a powerful text for preaching during Advent. It provides a context for exploring what it means to wait for God when routine threatens to extinguish visions of salvation. Furthermore, it explores the danger of pragmatism and outlines how the vision of salvation that is the end result of waiting must in fact be pulled back into the waiting period itself. The point of the prophet's message might be summarized as follows. The worshiping community does not have the luxury of questioning where divine justice might be found, because their very formation attests to its active role among humans. Given this fact, the questioning of divine justice by the people of God determines not its presence or absence but only its character. Will divine justice be the source of fiery purification for the people of God (v. 2-4) or judgment (v. 5)? Given divine justice in the midst of the people of God, we know that there is no such thing as mundane daily routine.

The Response: *Luke 1:68-79*

A Hymn of Praise or a Prophecy of Judgment?

Setting. Luke used hymns throughout the opening chapters of his Gospel to provide commentary on the events of Mary's conception (the Magnificat), the birth of John the Baptist (the Benedictus stated by Zechariah, the father of John), and the presentation of Jesus in the Temple (the Nunc Dimittis by Simeon). The Benedictus provides a response to the Old Testament lesson because Malachi 3:1 is referred to in Luke 1:76, where John the Baptist is interpreted as the messenger who will prepare the way for the Lord.

Structure. Luke 1:68-79 can be separated into two or three parts. Verses 68-75 are a hymn of praise, while vv. 76-79 are more prophetic in tone because Zechariah is pictured addressing John directly. One could break the structure into three parts by limiting the prophetic discourse to vv. 76-77, with the result that vv. 78-79 are interpreted as providing a summary and a conclusion to the song.

Significance. The Benedictus of Zechariah provides a response for Luke to the Old Testament lesson because it functions as fulfillment of prophecy. This line of interpretation pulls Malachi 2:17–3:5 more explicitly into the context of Christian Advent by reinterpreting the messenger of Malachi 3:1 as John. But this shift does not really answer the question of how the hymn provides a response. It only underscores how the Old Testament lesson is current for Christians. There are two responses to the Old Testament lesson depending on whether we focus on the singer, Zechariah, or on the baby, John. If the focus is on Zechariah then the hymn is the voice of those who are purified at the coming of God, who were described in Malachi 3:2-4. From this point of view Zechariah embodies the justice of God and now sings God's praise. If the focus shifts to John in the prophetic section, then the judgment of God's justice is accentuated through the role that this character will accept in preparing the way of Jesus. Here the images of judgment described in Malachi 3:5 come to the foreground. In other words, the song is a two-edged sword in much the same way as was the Old Testament lesson. How it is sung depends on whether or not justice informs the activity of the community of faith.

New Testament Texts

The readings from Philippians and Luke for this Second Sunday of Advent both use language that expresses a marked sense of anticipation in relation to God's future or forthcoming actions. Both texts are pointedly focused on the course of events in this world, and yet both passages show an awareness that God lays claim upon our present lives and calls them toward God's future which is qualitatively distinct from present reality.

The Epistle: *Philippians 1:3-11*

Living Life Toward "the Day of Christ"

Setting. The Philippian church was the first congregation on European soil that Paul founded. Through the years he seems to have maintained a very positive relationship with these particular converts. At the time he penned this letter Paul was in prison, and from statements made in the text we can see that he wrote to the Philippians for several reasons. These include: (1) to thank the Philippians for their support, physical and spiritual; (2) to discuss Epaphroditus's visit to him in behalf of the Philippians; and (3) to address difficulties and potential problems in the life of this particular church. The epistle reading for this week comes early in the letter, following the salutation (1:1-2) and preceding the body of the epistle (1:12–3:21); so that, specifically, 1:3-11 is the "thanksgiving" of the letter. The occurrence of the phrases "the day of Jesus Christ" (v. 6) and "the day of Christ" (v. 10) look forward and sound a note of anticipation that makes this passage an appropriate reading for the Advent season.

Structure. The thanksgiving of Philippians is a coherent section of the letter, but even in these nine verses one finds a rich complexity of statements. Verses 3-4 report Paul's regular, prayerful thanksgiving for the Philippians, and vv. 5 and 7 state the specific reasons for and contents of Paul's thankfulness. In the middle of these lines Paul declares his confidence that God will continue to work among the Philippians. And, finally vv. 8-11 communicate Paul's compassion and concern for the church in Philippi. Thus, we see this multifaceted "thanksgiving" expresses the ideas of prayer, joy, the mutual Christian experience of grace, confidence in God, compassion, concern, and anticipation; and these ideas, viewed particularly in terms of their interrelatedness in this passage, suggest motifs for proclamation.

Significance. Paul informs the Philippians that he is thankful in his memory for them and that he always expresses this thanks to God in his prayers. As one sees from vv. 5 and 7, the memory and the thanks are not merely the stuff of nebulous nostalgia; rather, Paul's joy over the Philippians and his thanks to God are for the consistent "sharing" of the Philippians in his ministry. Indeed, Paul's Greek makes the matter even clearer: He says the Philippians are "shareholders" (Greek, *sygkoinōnous*) with him in God's grace. Most likely, these verses are indirect references to the gifts that the Philippians sent to Paul as he was in prison (see 4:10-20). What is especially striking here is that between the statements about "sharing in the gospel" (v. 5) and having a mutual "share in God's grace" (v. 7) Paul declares his confidence that God will bring to completion the work among the Philippians that God had earlier begun.

We should notice that when Paul turns to God in prayer he does not merely engage in private personal piety. Paul's devotion to God is primarily vertical—that is, Paul understands God to be the source and the primary actor in all areas of life; but there is also a strong irrelinquishable horizontal dimension to Paul's prayer—that is, prayer is not simply a you-and-me affair, but a you-me-and-them engagement. Remarkably, when Paul turns to God he thinks of the Philippians and when Paul thinks of the Philippians he turns to God. The apostle understands that Christian life is lived out in terms of relationships, and he understands that in all Christian relations God is at work moving the mutual life of believers toward God's own appointed ends ("the day of Jesus Christ"). In other words, God's present work in the world is moving all of life toward God's goal of the future. And, now, those who relate to God in and through Jesus Christ have an understanding of who God is and who God calls us to be precisely because of the glimpse of God and the glimpse of true humanity given in Jesus Christ.

The Gospel: *Luke 3:1-6*

"All Flesh Shall See the Salvation of God!"

Setting. Luke's Gospel seems to start twice. Chapters 1–2 offer a formal historiographic prologue (1:1-4) and then go on to tell of the

Annunciation, birth, circumcision, naming, and prophetic declaration of John the Baptist and Jesus. Then one finds a further story about the boy Jesus. Chapter 3 could also serve as a beginning of Luke's story of Jesus, and indeed it begins to tell of Jesus' ministry at precisely the point that Mark opened his account of Jesus' work. Our reading comes immediately after the story of the boy Jesus in the Temple at the age of twelve. A bit later in chapter 3 (v. 23) Luke tells us that "Jesus was about thirty years old when he began his work," so that our reading comes after a leap of at least eighteen years through story time. Luke carefully sets his story in this new temporal location. In fact, 3:1-22 is a kind of narrative prologue to the account of the ministry of the adult Jesus. Our reading is the opening portion of this section of the Gospel.

Structure. Luke composed the lines of our reading so that they unfold in three stages. First, vv. 1-2 set the narrative in relation to "world history" (as Luke and his readers knew the world). The references to the governmental structures of the Roman world, especially focusing on Palestine, place the story in a grand frame that suggests the universal significance of the story (an idea stated explicitly in v. 6). At the end of v. 2 we meet John the son of Zechariah (better known to us as John the Baptist). He is a familiar figure to those who have read the first two chapters of Luke's account, and now Luke needs only to place John in the wilderness. Then, second, v. 3 tells us of the adult John's ministry. Third, in vv. 4-6 Luke, as the narrator of the account, offers a citation from "the book of the words of the prophet Isaiah" which actually explains the person and the purpose of John's work.

Significance. Because of the explicit parallel imperatives of v. 4, "Prepare the way of the Lord, make his paths straight," and the future tenses of the verbs ("shall be filled," "shall be made low," "shall be made straight," and "shall see") this passage issues a strong call to preparation and expectation, so that this lesson is well-suited to Advent. Still other features of the text suggest lines for preaching in the context of this season. First, the careful way in which Luke locates this story in time and place shows that the Christian gospel is a message of world significance. The structures of human life exist in the plain sight of God and are fully accountable to the one whom this passage calls "Lord." Despite the seemingly godless form of the foundation, framework, and façade of much of modern "secular" life, John's voice in the wilderness reminds us that even the most desolate areas of the world are part of a creation that is the concern of the Creator. When we come upon a passage like this in the Advent season we are reminded that God stands over all of this world, so the shape and substance of our own religion, supposedly being recharged with expectation in these weeks prior to Christmas, must necessarily be related to the realities of life in this world, not merely focused falsely on a distant God who is the object of insulated piety.

Furthermore, Luke explains that John's ministry was one of calling people to repentance and baptism—an altered life and a symbol of the grace that forgives us our sins and thereby enables the transformation of our existence. During Advent we celebrate our expectation—but expectation of what? Of Jesus' birth? He has already been born, and long ago. Of Jesus' second coming? Already in the power and presence of the Holy Spirit we believe he has come to us, so that his "second" coming will mark God's judgment on the end of our earthly time—not merely return our long absent Lord to us. No, we expect God's grace in the sense of yearning for (1) that which we have already experienced and (2) that which we know enables us to live ever differently from our formerly sinful ways.

Finally, with the lines from Isaiah (40:3-5) Luke interprets the person and the work of the Baptist. He is a herald of the coming of the Lord. He calls people to prepare for the coming of the Lord. Yet, these lines say more about the Lord than they do about the Baptist. Not only are the verbs cast in the future, several are formed in the passive voice; so that it is absolutely clear that human beings are not the subjects of these verbs, rather God is. In context, Luke uses these verses from Isaiah to show how John called people to prepare for the coming of Jesus in his earthly ministry; but the lines themselves transcend their context and declare the power and the purpose of God. God—who has the power to level valleys, mountains, and hills, to straighten the crooked, and to smooth the rough—God is the one who brings salvation to all humankind. God's concern, God's call, and God's work is ultimately for the salvation of humans, all humans. But, what is this "salvation"? It is helpful to know that in Greek, salvation (*sōtēria*) can mean "deliverance," "preservation," and "way of safety"; and this noun is related to a verb (Greek, *sōzō*) which means "to save from death" and "to keep alive." In short, the text tells us to expect God to do what is necessary for our well-being. In the rest of the Gospel as we follow Jesus through the course of his ministry, we learn more precisely the nature of God's provisions for the salvation of humankind.

Advent 2: The Celebration

Those who work out of the officially published form of the *Revised Common Lectionary* (Nashville: Abingdon Press, 1992) will note that for this Sunday it lists, from the Apocrypha, Baruch 5:1-9 as the First Lesson. Malachi 3:1-4 is listed in second place as an alternative. Because it is assumed that most of our readership is from traditions that do not use the Apocrypha on any regular basis, we have elected to do our commentary above on the Malachi passage.

The Malachi 3 selection may not be appropriate unless certain tensions are acknowledged. The text of Malachi appears, given the Gospel reading, to be intended as a reference to John the Baptist ("I am sending my messenger to prepare the way before me"), but the rest of the passage has been heard by the Church as referring to the work of Christ, not John. This same passage is used as the Gospel reading on the Feast of the Presentation of Christ in the Temple (Feb. 2) because of the line after that quoted above, "the Lord whom you seek will suddenly come to his temple." The passage concerns judgment, but it is the judgment that only Christ can bring on the day of the Lord, even if John can prepare the people for that judgment.

Another choice for this day might be Malachi 4:1-6. Verse 6 is used in Luke 1:17 to refer specifically to John the Baptist. The first part of Malachi 4 has the ring of John's preaching without possibly confusing his call to repentance with that of Christ's call. The Advent image of the rising of the sun of righteousness is also to be found in this chapter.

The references to the "day of Jesus Christ" in Philippians, combined with the ongoing theme of repentance in the Gospel reading, and the day of the Lord theme in Malachi make R.B.Y. Scott's hymn, "O Day of God, Draw Nigh" an appropriate choice as a bridge between the epistle and Gospel readings. Included in many hymnals, it can also be found in the following new denominational books: Baptist, no. 623; Episcopal, nos. 600-1; Presbyterian, no. 452; United Methodist, no. 730.

The response to the first lesson, Luke 1:68-79, is the Canticle or Song of Zechariah, also known as the Benedictus. In the Anglican tradition it has been appointed for use at Morning Prayer as the response to the New Testament lesson, and it is employed daily in the Morning Prayer Liturgy of the Roman Catholic Church. Metrical versions of it for congregational singing may be found in *Hymnal: A Worship Book* (Brethren and Mennonite, 1992), no. 174; *The Baptist Hymnal* (1991), no. 79; *The Hymnal 1982* (Episcopal), no. 444; *The Presbyterian Hymnal* (1990), nos. 601-2; *The United Methodist Hymnal* (1989), no. 209; and *Worship: A Hymnal and Service Book for Roman Catholics* (1986), no. 6.

Third Sunday of Advent

Old Testament Texts

Both Zephaniah 3:14-20 and Isaiah 12:2-6 are songs of salvation that follow extended oracles of judgment against Israel.

The Lesson: *Zephaniah 3:14-20*

God's Hymn of Salvation

Setting. The superscription to the book places the oracles of Zephaniah toward the end of the seventh century B.C.E. If we take the superscription as the historical and social context for interpreting the book, then it would appear that Zephaniah broke a long prophetic silence with his words of judgment during the early reign of King Josiah (640–609 B.C.E.), since the last prophetic voices indicated in the Old Testament were those of Isaiah and Micah at the close of the eighth century B.C.E. One reason to account for the lack of prophesy during the period between Isaiah/Micah and Zephaniah was the strong rule of Assyria during the early and middle part of the seventh century B.C.E. There was not a great deal of room for a distinctive Yahwistic voice when Judah was a vassal to Assyria. The predominance of the oracles of judgment in Zephaniah regarding the worship of the people (1:4-6) and the leadership of the king (vv. 8-9) may be an indication of a reform spirit that is associated with King Josiah in 621 B.C.E.

Structure. The concluding hymn can be separated in a number of different ways. It includes much of the imagery of enthronement psalms (e.g., Psalms 47, 95, 97), where God is celebrated as ruling over Israel as a king who has ascended a throne. From this perspective note how the song begins with an imperative to praise God, "Sing aloud!" (v. 14), which is followed by statements about how

God reigns as king (v. 15), how this brings assurance (v. 16), because the Lord is victorious over enemies (v. 17), and that because of this there will be peace and security (vv. 18-20). Another way to separate the psalm is to note the shift from third person references to God in vv. 14-17 to first person reference in vv. 18-20. From this perspective the first half of the psalm is an announcement describing the fact of God's enthronement in the Temple, which implies forgiveness. The primary motif of this section is stated in vv. 15 and 17 ("The king of Israel, the LORD is in your midst."). Once this reality has been established, first person divine speech takes over for the remainder of the song in vv. 18-20 where no less than eight promises are made by God. These promises are the content of the divine song that is noted at the close of v. 17.

Significance. The correspondence between Zephaniah 3:14-20 and other Enthronement Psalms invites an interpretation that places the song within the larger context of Day-of-the-Lord imagery. The references in v. 20 of "At that time" suggest such imagery as the Day of the Lord within the song, which is also reinforced in the larger context of the book (1:14). The danger of preaching the concluding song in isolation from the larger context of the book is that the two-sidedness of the Day of the Lord is lost.

Zephaniah 3:14-20 is certainly a strong statement of salvation and praise at the close of the book, but this proclamation of salvation must be placed in the larger context of Zephaniah, where oracles of judgment predominate. An overview of the book will illustrate the point. The book opens with judgment oracles first against the nations (1:2-3) and then against Judah (1:4-6), before the image of the Day of the Lord takes over in 1:7 where judgment continues to be the primary message. The Day of the Lord will be a time of wrath against the king, princes, and all persons "who rest complacently on their dregs, those who say in their hearts, 'The LORD will not do good, nor will he do harm.' " (1:12). The motif here is of the syrupy substance (dregs) created by fermentation of wine (lees), from which clear wine is poured off. In other words, the prophet accuses Judah of becoming so numb (so syrupy and dull) to the presence of God that they neither believe nor disbelieve. Such indifference in the shadow of the Temple where God was enthroned left Israel hopeless, according to the prophet. Judgment, therefore, continues to be the primary focus through chapter 2 and in the beginning of chapter 3, first on the nations (2:4-14) and then on Jerusalem (3:1-8). But the mood begins to switch in 3:9-20 to salvation as a process of purification after judgment. Two oracles of salvation are described in 3:9-13 (note the use of "At that time" and "On that day" in vv. 9 and 11), which provide the immediate context for the concluding song of salvation which is the Old Testament lesson.

There is a strong Advent sermon in Zephaniah. One never doubts throughout this prophetic book that God will indeed be enthroned in the midst of the people. In doubt, however, is what effect the enthronement of God will have on those in the vicinity of God. It could be the source of judgment or salvation. A variety of dangers are listed by the prophet in the opening chapters as actions that will determine whether the enthronement of God will occasion a song or a cry (e.g., exploitative behavior, violence, fraud), but perhaps the most striking is indifference, which is explored through the imagery of dregs of wine. Whatever images may be used to describe the function of Advent within the Christian year, indifference certainly cannot be one of them, because of the inevitability of Christmas as the culmination of our waiting for God to be present in our midst. When viewed in this way, there is a correlation between Christmas and the Day of the Lord—both will inevitably happen. What is not clear in each case is whether the presence of God in the midst of the people of God will occasion judgment or a song of salvation. Zephaniah serves as a strong wake-up call in the middle of Advent. It underscores how waiting is an active quality informed by expectations of an inevitable end result—the enthronement of God in the midst of the people of God. Waiting in this case embodies a whole range of moral characteristics, which then function as our ticket to the sanctuary on Christmas.

The Response: *Isaiah 12:2-6*

The Community's Hymn of Salvation

Setting. Isaiah 12:2-6 includes many of the motifs about salvation that arose in Zephaniah 3:14-20. In fact some scholars would classify both as eschatological hymns of salvation. The strongest point of comparison occurs in Isaiah 12:6 where the royal imagery of Zion reappears and God is confessed as being in the midst of Israel. A careful reading of the remainder of the psalm, however, yields little correspondence to Zephaniah. The main difference between the two songs is the predominance of Exodus motifs in Isaiah, where God is confessed as the psalmist's salvation, strength, and might (see the same motifs in Exodus 15:1-2).

Structure. The lectionary text does not include Isaiah 12:1, which places the hymn in vv. 2-6 within the larger setting of a divine reversal from wrath to comfort. Verses 2-6 separate into three parts: v. 2 is a statement of praise with the reason for praise, vv. 3-4 describe a liturgical procession with water and the liturgy that must accompany it, and vv. 5-6 conclude the song with an invitation to praise.

Significance. Isaiah 12:(1) 2-6 complements Zephaniah 3:14-20 in a number of ways. First, both texts describe the presence of God in the Temple as an occasion of salvation. Second, a brief reading of Isaiah 1–12 would also underscore how the hymn of praise for the salvation of God in Isaiah 12:(1) 2-6 also occurs in the larger context of divine judgment against the people of God in Isaiah 1–11. Verse 1 underscores this reversal and thus should probably be included in the reading. The larger context of Isaiah underscores continuity in the emphasis on the two-sided character of God's presence that was also important for preaching Zephaniah. Third, the song of Isaiah 12:(1) 2-6 also provides an important point of contrast to Zephaniah 3:14-20 that is worth exploring in preaching these texts, or in using Isaiah 12(1) 2-6 within the liturgy. Zephaniah 3:14-20 was a hymn about the salvation of God from God's point of view. It began with a Temple priest or some other cultic person preparing the community for the enthronement of God in the Temple (1:14-17), which then gave way to an extended divine speech (1:18-20). Isaiah 12:(1) 2-6, on the other hand, is the voice of the worshiping community. The "I" of this hymn is the worshiper who now responds to the event of God's enthronement and the promises of divine deliverance that accompany it. Three things are noteworthy about the language of the worshiper for using this psalm in worship. The first is the central place of praise, the second is the importance of Exodus imagery to articulate praise to God, and the third are the directions for liturgical action as a means of praising God. The final point in particular encourages creative reflection on how this responsive hymn of praise might be used within the liturgy of the worship service.

New Testament Texts

Again the readings come from Philippians and Luke. Paul offers practical spiritual advice in the epistle, and John the Baptist tells his hearers in specific terms how they are to live in demonstration of their repentance. Neither text, however, can be viewed as mere moral teaching; for in both readings we find a strong eschatological note. Paul declares, "The Lord is near"; and John says, "The ax is lying at the root of the trees," and, then, he prophesies, "One who is more powerful than I is coming." These eschatological elements are not merely trappings of the past that may be disregarded or translated into seemingly more "realistic" categories. Indeed, they articulate a worldview with which we must come to terms in order to preach these passages with integrity.

The Epistle: *Philippians 4:4-7*

The Shape and Substance of Life in Christ

Setting. Much of Paul's essentially friendly letter to the Philippians is practical in nature. Throughout the epistle he offers the congregation helpful advice about their life in Christ (for example, see 1:27–2:18 and 3:2-21). Nevertheless, the verses of the reading are even more pointedly practical. In this passage Paul moves from the level of general, helpful remarks to give specific instructions about specific issues in the life of the congregation. The statement in v. 5, "The Lord is near," suggests the use of this portion of Philippians during Advent.

Structure. The reading occurs in the midst of several relatively independent pieces of advice that are brought together in 4:1-9. This larger section opens with the word "therefore" (4:1), which demonstrates that all that will follow is related to Paul's explicit admoni-

45

tions in the previous verses (3:14, 21). There he told the Philippians to press on toward the goal of "the heavenly call of God in Christ Jesus" with full confidence in Jesus Christ, who has "the power . . . to make all things subject to himself." In this context, Paul twice states a command to "rejoice" (v. 4) and, then, continues with further pieces of "spiritual" advice in vv. 5-7.

Significance. Recognize the basis of the instructions that Paul issues in these verses. The opening word of v. 1, "therefore," sets the apostle's directions on the foundation of the preceding words of encouragement in 3:12-21, especially vv. 15-21. The power to accomplish what Paul instructs the Philippians to do is not simply their own efforts and energies; rather they live and work together in the context of the power of the Lord Jesus Christ, who, as the Savior, will transform the Philippians into his own likeness.

Seldom does so much of Paul's deep affection for a congregation come through in his remarks as it does in 4:1. Yet, even this is not mere fondness, but genuine Christian devotion, which is clear from Paul's use of the phrase, "in the Lord."

Verses 4-7 move to a lofty level of reflection and direction as Paul describes the activities and characteristics of Christian life: rejoicing, gentleness, lack of anxiety, prayer, thanksgiving, and peace. Consultation of more in-depth commentaries and a good theological dictionary will reward those who wish to develop these words into themes for preaching. Yet, other approaches to the passage are possible. To illustrate: Notice in these statements the context of Christian life: "in the Lord" (4:4); the motivation of this life: "the Lord is near" (4:5); the orientation of such a life: "to God" (4:6); and the source of such a life: "of God" (4:7). Thus, while the characteristics listed above are suggestive for preaching, perhaps a fuller treatment of this text will deal with Christian life, its characteristics, context, motivation, orientation, and source. For Advent proclamation stressing the "motivation" ("the Lord is near") may prove beneficial. From start to finish the preacher should remember, and in the preaching remind the congregation, that Christian life is not lived as a job to be performed, but as a privilege to be experienced in relation to the person and the power of the Lord Jesus Christ. Far from telling the Philippians merely to relax and enjoy living, Paul directs them to an active life of faith that is anxiety-free because of the presence and power of the Lord.

The Gospel: *Luke 3:7-18*

The Promise of God's Future

Setting. Our reading for this week immediately follows the verses of last week's Gospel lesson, so readers may wish to consult the discussion of setting for the Second Sunday of Advent. Last week we simply met John the Baptist, and Luke used a citation from Isaiah to inform the reader about the significance of John. This week we move into more direct contact with John, hearing his preaching and teaching as we see him interact with the people who came out to hear his message and to be baptized.

Structure. The verses of the lesson take in a complex of materials. In fact, there are four distinct units in the reading. Verses 7-9 recall the bold preaching of John to the crowds, and vv. 10-14 are a report of three exchanges between John and different groups that put questions to the Baptist. In turn, vv. 15-17 record John's "answer" to the christological curiosity of the people, offering a prophetic declaration concerning the coming Mightier One. Finally, v. 18 actually begins a new unit (vv. 18-20), which is clear from the Greek grammatical construction that frames v. 18; it is only the first part of a larger ("on the one hand . . . on the other hand") statement. By placing v. 18 with vv. 7-17 the lectionary makes it function as a summarizing statement in relation to all that John says in these verses.

Significance. All John's words have a prophetic ring, not merely because of their future cast, but inherent in the bold manner in which they articulate a call to godly living is the clear recognition of God's authority over all of human life. The strong words of vv. 7-9 are a pure prophetic vituperation! By calling the crowd "you brood of vipers" John does more than engage in insult and name-calling. He confronts the people with the danger of self-deception. Since humans are "as sneaky as a snake" it is possible that they can present themselves for baptism merely as if they were taking out an insurance policy. John's theological common sense recognizes that "actions speak louder than words," so that the best indicator of real repentance is an altered life. John calls for real change and evidence of it. This is not works righteousness (the great Protestant fear!), but a recognition that true faith generates godly efforts (not seeing this truth is the great Protestant heresy!). John warns his hearers against the smug self-assurance of heredity, for faith lives anew in each generation; and recognizing God's authority, John declares God's indifference to human systems of security. The metaphor of judgment in v. 9 has an eschatological ring, so that we should understand that the promise of future divine judgment calls us to an appropriately altered life at present.

The next section (vv. 10-14) follows the warning, so that we see three different groups taking John's preaching seriously. We do not have a catalogue of "all righteousness" here, rather the character of the particular group determines or influences the particular response concerning "what we should do." If the particular congregation addressed by a preacher is analogous to one or more of these groups, the preaching may take its cues rather directly from the text; but should a preacher face an assembly of poor farmers, homeless people, and abused spouses, it will be necessary to extrapolate from the dynamics of the text in relation to those persons' situations in order to speak about "what we should do." John calls the first group away from pure self-interest to genuine generosity through concern for others. The tax collectors are called to honesty and fair dealings. (Perhaps consulting a Bible dictionary regarding the Roman tax system will assist in reflecting on this text.) Notice, however, that John did not tell these people to stop collecting taxes. Radical as John was, he called people to God, not to anarchy. Implicit in John's remarks is a recognition of the responsibility of taxpayers to support the structures that afford them social benefits; yet, more directly, he calls on those who operate "the system" to act responsibly. The final group, the soldiers, are called away from an abuse of power and to contentment rather than tyrannical greed.

The third unit of material, vv. 15-17, takes the spotlight off John the Baptist. John's declarations reveal that his own responsible labor is as a witness to the forthcoming actions of God which, as we learn from Luke's account, are focused in Jesus Christ. John promises judgment, but we should never forget the surprising manner in which God's judgment was revealed—first, as a babe ¦ then, through a bold ministry of compassion; and finally, through the revelation of the depth of God's love in Jesus' death on a cross. The dazzling power of God brought Jesus' resurrection, which was the clearest confirmation of the will and authority of God revealed in the person and work of Jesus Christ. Although v. 18 is cast in this reading in the role of a summary, we should take a careful look at the verse. John's warnings and promises can be heard as terrible threats, and indeed the strong language should grasp our attention. But notice how in v. 18 Luke tells us the Baptist's preaching was "good news." This powerful lesson should inform us that God does have standards and that God evaluates human life in relation to those divine values. But, rather than merely threaten, John's words call us to change, and in doing so they declare the "good news" that altered lives are realities, not merely wishes.

Advent 3: The Celebration

The response to the first lesson, the First Song of Isaiah, is available in various choral editions. It can also be found in a metrical version by Carl P. Daw., Jr., in the Episcopal *The Hymnal 1982*, nos. 678-79.

The two following Charles Wesley stanzas provide a positive response to the Gospel reading on this Gaudete Sunday. The reading is so severe in tone that it is possible to miss what seems to be a non sequitur—namely, that Luke summarizes the Baptist's call to repentance as a proclamation of "good news to the people." The liturgy here has the same pattern as in the first lesson and its response, where in each case the good news of salvation follows upon the proclamation of judgment (see commentary above).

> Jesus comes with all his grace,
> Comes to save a fallen race:
> Object of our glorious hope,
> Jesus comes to lift us up.

> Let the living stones cry out;
> Let the seed of Abram shout,
> Praise we all our lowly King,
> Give him thanks, rejoice, and sing.

49

The first stanza could be used to introduce the Gospel reading and the second be a response to it. Either the tune Innocents or Savannah would be appropriate if the stanzas are being used separately. If used as one stanza of eight lines, Llanfair (with an Alleluia after each line) would underscore the theme of rejoicing on this day.

The epistle reading today provided the basis for the traditional benediction, "The peace of God which passes all understanding. . . ." It may be adapted for the dismissal and blessing today, as follows:

> Go forth rejoicing in the promise of salvation.
> And the peace of God, which surpasses all understanding,
> guard your hearts and minds in Christ Jesus today and always.

Some similar form, based upon the reading, may be used to introduce or provide the formula for the exchange of the Peace. The two may be combined by incorporating the Peace as part of the final blessing, so that people are encouraged to greet one another in the Peace of the Lord as they prepare to leave.

The emphasis on peace here also suggests the use of the carol "It Came upon the Midnight Clear," if not in whole, at least the stanza beginning, "For lo! the days are hastening on," as a response to the epistle reading. Or that stanza may be used after the passing of the Peace, wherever it occurs in the service.

Fourth Sunday of Advent

Old Testament Texts

Micah 2:2-5*a* is an oracle of salvation about a future ruler. Luke 1:46*b*-55 is Mary's song of praise known as the Magnificat, which she sings in response to becoming pregnant with Jesus.

The Lesson: *Micah 2:2-5*a

An Oracle of Salvation

Setting. The superscription to the book of Micah places the prophet at the close of the eighth century B.C.E., and it states that his audience was both the northern and the southern kingdoms. Whether Micah prophesied in the north is difficult to say. Yet the fall of the northern kingdom with its capital of Samaria in 722 B.C.E. is a central event in the background, which is actually referred to in 1:6-7. Micah also appears to make reference to the invasion of the Assyrian king Sennacherib in 701 B.C.E. (1:10-16) and perhaps the reforms of Hezekiah (715–687 B.C.E.) during this same period of time (2:6). An explicit association of Micah with Hezekiah is made in the book of Jeremiah (chapter 26), which suggests that there was indeed a tradition of Micah with this king, even though Isaiah is usually the prophet associated with Hezekiah. The language and imagery of the book suggest that the prophet embodied southern tradition which emphasized the presence of God in the Jerusalem Temple (1:2-3) and the choice of the Davidic line as king (5:1-4).

Structure. Scholars debate just how the book of Micah is organized and how much of the book should be attributed to the prophet. The reader is encouraged to pursue these problems in other commentaries. Two points concerning structure are important for purposes of preaching Micah 5:2-5*a*, and they will be our point of focus. The first concerns the larger structure of the book as the context in which to interpret Micah 5:2-5a. Three times in the book of Micah the command "to hear" is put forward by the prophet. In 2:2 the peoples are commanded to hear, in 3:1 the heads of Jacob and rulers of Israel are commanded to hear (NRSV, "listen," see also 3:9), and in 6:1 there is a call for the mountains to hear God's legal controversy with Israel (probably for the purpose of functioning as witnesses in the trial). These indicators suggest that one way to separate the book is in three parts. Chapters 1–2 are made up primarily of judgment oracles against Israel for their worship practices (1:7) and their social injustices (2:1-2, 8-9). The section concludes with a small glimpse of salvation in 2:12-13. Chapters 3–5 begin with additional oracles of judgment (chapter 3), before switching to an extended section of salvation (chapters 4–5). Chapters 6–7 close the book by presenting a combination of judgment and salvation oracles. The larger outline of the book underscores how the salvation oracle of 5:2-5a is actually meant to function in the larger context of judgment. Second, the insight from context raises questions about the boundaries of the lectionary text. Most scholars would agree that the description of siege warfare in 5:1 should be included with the unit. The inclusion of this verse underscores the mixture of judgment and salvation that is characteristic of the larger book, which is absent if the boundaries of the text are limited to 5:2-5a.

Significance. Micah 5:2 is quoted in Matthew 2:6 as a prophecy about the birth of a future Messiah, who is Jesus. The story line in the Gospel begins with Herod meeting the wise men who are looking for a newborn child destined to be king of the Jews. This news unnerves Herod, who then asks the chief priests and scribes where the Messiah was to be born, to which they respond by quoting Micah 5:2. He will be born in Bethlehem. The use of Micah 5:2 in Matthew raises the following question for preaching: How do you preach Micah 5:(1) 2-5a when you have such a strong and explicit interbiblical connection, which is reinforced even further by having the Magnificat as the psalm response? Biblical scholars have tended to go in two directions at this point. One avenue interprets Micah 5:(1) 2-5a as a proof text for the authenticity of Jesus as the Messiah. This tends to be labeled as a conservative perspective in contemporary scholarship because prophecy is interpreted as pointing primarily to Jesus. The problem with this approach is that once the connection between a prophetic text and its fulfillment in Jesus is made, little else needs to be stated. Another preacher might propose that Micah 5:(1) 2-5a must be read in its own right, within the historical horizons of the eighth-century prophet. This tends to be labeled a more liberal and critical perspective because the links between Micah and Jesus are diminished. The problem with this approach is that once Micah 5:(1) 2-5a is interpreted independently it becomes difficult to reestablish the connection between Micah and Matthew that the Gospel writer has encouraged.

The preacher need not make a choice between these two perspectives, for they can in fact become complementary forms of interpretation, but the order in which the two different methods are used is important. Interpretation should begin with the second or critical perspective. The central question from this perspective is: How does the oracle of salvation function within the book of Micah? Our early conclusions under structure are important at this point. The book of Micah is a mixture of judgment and salvation oracles. The mixing of genres suggests that the presence of God is a two-edged sword in the book. What appears powerful and secure (Jerusalem, the hierarchy associated with the king and the priesthood) is the object of judgment oracles by the prophet, because such attribution of security is a form of idolatry. Consequently the appearance of God in Jerusalem is one of judgment, because God will unmask false forms of security and power. Salvation or reliable security, on the other hand, is located by the prophet in Bethlehem of Ephrathah, which from appearance would be judged insignificant as compared to Jerusalem. Is Micah thinking about Jesus in making this contrast between appearance and reality with regard to power and security when he mentions Bethlehem? Certainly not. Micah 5:1 links this passage back to current political and religious problems in Judah, which is one reason why this verse should be included in the pericope. The contrasts about power and security, however, raise larger issues that are true to the life of faith at different times and places.

By quoting Micah 5:(1) 2-5a Matthew uses the contrasts about power and security in Micah as a stage for interpreting the birth of

Jesus. The interbiblical connection provides a transition from Advent to Christmas that can be explored in preaching by raising the following question: How does our understanding of Micah 5:(1) 2-5a enrich our reading of the birth of Jesus? A variety of comparisons can be pursued at this point. The most obvious is the contrast about power and security. Matthew is probing this issue by contrasting the powerful and seemingly secure Herod in Jerusalem with the seemingly powerless infant Jesus, who is born in Bethlehem. This contrast leads into a second. Micah 5:(1) 2-5a was an affirmation of hope in a Messiah when the present situation of siege warfare by Assyria would lead Judah to deny such a hope. Matthew frames the birth of Jesus in a similar context of siege in which Herod replaces the Assyrians, in his desire to kill the infant. These comparisons begin to illustrate how Micah 5:(1) 2-5a (1) provides a wide range of commentary on the birth of Jesus, and (2) how the text also presents a challenge to present communities of faith to affirm God's messianic salvation in similar contexts of threat, when such promises are not necessarily being experienced.

The Response: *Luke 1:47-55*

A Psalm of Thanksgiving

Setting. The Magnificat underscores how the life of faith is filled with many reversals so that what appears to be secure frequently is not. Mary celebrates her pregnancy by underscoring how the inbreaking of God can frequently bring the powerful down, while lifting the humble to higher positions. This contrast is very similar to the comparison of Jerusalem and Bethlehem in Micah 5:(1) 2-5a as well as Jesus and Herod.

Structure. The song separates into four parts: an introduction of thanks (v. 47), a recounting of personal experience (vv. 48-49), confession (vv. 50-53), and a thank-offering with confidence (vv. 54-55).

Significance. Luke uses Mary's experience of reversal (which may be her barrenness and then subsequent pregnancy, or more likely her having been chosen by God to bear Jesus even though she was of low social status) to explore how this is characteristic of God's salvation in all contexts. The confessional section of the song explores this larger issue by comparing and contrasting the reversals between the strong and the weak, and the rich and the poor at the hands of God. The point of the Magnificat is very similar to the prophet Micah. The inbreaking of God is a two-edged sword. It can bring down the proud who thought they were secure in their power, while it can also locate power in surprising places by raising up the weak.

New Testament Texts

These challenging texts bring the proclamation of Advent to a dramatic conclusion. The difficult text from Hebrews calls Christians to the recognition that Christ's coming means that, in our devotion to God, we must and can move beyond compromises that dilute our faith. In turn, the beautiful lesson from Luke tells of the depths of God's grace and the joy of experiencing the transformation of our lives through that grace.

The Epistle: *Hebrews 10:5-10*

The Consequence of the Coming of Christ

Setting. Although Hebrews opens like a treatise, it proceeds like a sermon, and it closes like a letter. The whole of Hebrews is an elaborate discourse on the superiority of Jesus Christ and the meaning of being a person of Christian faith. The entirety of Hebrews is written in the tones of a grand exhortation that is designed to encourage the readers to have something more than nominal faith and to live something more than an aimless life. The verses for this Sunday are a part of the sermonic proceedings of the writing, and they are situated toward the end of the third major section of Hebrews (8:1–10:18) which focuses on Christ's death.

Structure. Discerning the structure of these verses is a key to their interpretation. Verse 5 is an introductory line leading into a modified citation of Psalm 39:7-9 (in the Septuagint, English Psalm 40) in vv. 5b-7. Next, vv. 8-9 offer exegesis of the quotation; then, v. 10 applies the interpretation to the readers or hearers of Hebrews. This kind of scriptural exposition was the norm in first-century Judaism and Christianity, though the shape and substance of the passage

55

(especially the author's casual manner of altering the quotation) seem foreign to many of us today.

The basic assumptions and statements that the author makes in the course of this passage are themselves suggestive for proclamation: (1) Christ came into the world; (2) Christ speaks through Scripture; (3) Christ reveals the uselessness of mere religious ritual and the necessity of doing God's will; (4) Christ himself lived out God's will; and (5) through the life and work of Christ, including especially his atoning death, Christians are given a new relationship to God.

Significance. Most interpreters understand that in its original historical context Hebrews was written to Jewish Christians who were experiencing difficulties that caused them to have a nostalgic longing for the security of the synagogue that they enjoyed before their conversion to Christianity. Thus, the letter is a strong statement about the sufficiency, indeed the superiority, of Christ. When the letter polemicizes against the law and sacrificial system of the Jewish cult, it is arguing against the urge of Christians to return to Judaism; it is not polemicizing directly against Judaism itself.

In the context of the Advent season, this text stands out because of the words of the opening line, "Consequently, when Christ came into the world. . . . " The idea of Christ's coming more than anything else makes this text "at home" in Advent. The coming here is clearly Christ's "first" coming, as the NRSV makes clear with the simple past tense verb "came," although in Greek the verb is present tense (not future!). The focus on the "coming" deals with what Christ said (vv. 5-8), what he did (v. 9), and what it means (v. 10).

Exegetically oriented preaching done with hermeneutical sophistication requires some reflection on these two "contexts" in conjunction with one another—and in conjunction with the make-up and life of the particular congregation where the preaching will be done. The first thing to note is that this text is not a license to go about bashing Jews; its concern is with Jewish Christians. In turn, only the rare congregation today will be composed of Jewish converts to Christianity, especially ones who are feeling tempted to return to the synagogue. And so, how can we use this text? Think about the congregation to which the sermon will be delivered. What is it about the lives of the people in the church that tempt them away from strong Christian commitments? What lures them away from Christ, especially in an offer of serenity? This text tells us that Christ has made such pre-Christian systems of security meaningless, for in giving himself to do God's will he establishes the reality of godliness at all costs.

In the world today this passage tells us that the coming of Christ means that God has laid an ultimate claim on our lives. All other worldly standards have been relativized, marginalized, and even undone. This is a daring message, as Christ's giving of his very life was a daring act. For contemporary Christians, this text tells us that Christ calls us and enables us to live our lives daringly for God.

The Gospel: *Luke 1:39-45 (46-55)*

Perceiving and Praising God's Grace

Setting. Through the course of this Advent season we have backed our way through the gospel according to Luke by moving from Jesus' teachings about the future, through the time of the outset of his ministry, now to the period prior to his birth. The continuity of the season is enforced by the theme of coming or expectation rather than in any progressively linear sense. This week's lesson actually presupposes some familiarity with the story told in Luke 1:5-38, where the forthcoming (miraculous) births of both John the Baptist and Jesus were foretold by angels. With the expectation that is set by these important births, our lesson tells of the visit of Mary to the home of Elizabeth and Zechariah.

Structure. The primary lectionary reading focuses on the story of Mary's visit and the exclamation of Elizabeth at her arrival, and the possible secondary reading includes the celebrated declaration of Mary, the Magnificat. Whether one treats vv. 39-45 or vv. 39-55 as the text, the dynamics are the same. First, the story tells of "divinely inspired recognition" (vv. 39-41*a*); and, then, of "divinely inspired praise" (vv. 41*b*-45 or vv. 41*b*-55). Obviously these themes may (should) inform the proclamation of either the first or the second form of the lesson.

Significance. As simple as the themes suggested above seem to be, the text tells us a profound truth about the grace of God. Both the capacity to recognize God's work in Jesus Christ and the expression of praise to God for that work are gifts from God. The words of the angel to Zechariah concerning the as yet unconceived John foretold that "even before his birth he [would] be filled with the Holy Spirit" (1:15), and in our lesson vv. 41b-42a say, "And Elizabeth was filled with the Holy Spirit and exclaimed with a loud cry. . . . " The Spirit of God endows humanity with the eyes of faith to see and the voice of faith to sing God's praises.

A brief excursion along a side-path is in order: In Psalm 42:7 as the psalmist ponders the majesty of God we read, "Deep calls to deep at the thunder of your cataracts"; so that in poetry we find the faith perception expressed in both the story and the poetry of our Gospel lesson for this week. We should recognize that a persistent element of biblical faith and biblical theology is that God's own thorough, gracious involvement with human life and creation is itself the source of creation's capacity to recognize and praise the divine.

Thus, the story of the visit of Mary to Elizabeth is a subtle but sophisticated reminder that we are able to relate to God through the person and work of Jesus Christ because of God's own graciousness in relating to us. Advent is a season of expectation. And this wonderful story tells us that our lives are to be as pregnant as were Mary and Elizabeth with the expectation of the transforming experience of God's grace.

A careful look at our text tells us something of the nature of God's grace. Grace has to do with the Lordship of Jesus Christ. Grace has to do with joy. Grace means salvation, for God is concerned with those whose needs are so profound that they can do nothing other than depend upon the Lord. Grace means mercy, and that of a quality that it cannot be exhausted through time. Grace is the essence of God's faithfulness.

One dimension of this text that may prove difficult, but which should not be avoided, is the way in which God's grace is understood to "scatter the proud," to "bring down the powerful," and to "send the rich away empty." The news that the hungry will be filled with good things sounds promising by itself, but in this text God's loving care is coupled with the celebration of the demise of the upper echelons of the status quo. The text is neither a call to an egalitarian ethic nor a license for militant behavior, rather it is a radical recognition of the power of *God* to reverse the fortunes of this world. Humans do not have final authority over their lives, God does. And, as the text sings of God's ways, it informs us both of who God is and who in Jesus Christ he calls us to be. Finally, the experience of grace, as the capacity to recognize God's work and the ability to utter God's praise, must inform a life that embodies God's values.

Advent 4: The Celebration

In order to avoid repetition in today's service, planners should note that, if the Magnificat is used as the response to the Old Testament lesson, the longer version of the Gospel reading should not be used because it is the account of the Magnificat. If the longer Gospel reading is used, then Psalm 80:1-7 or some other response (such as the last stanza of "O Little Town of Bethlehem") will more appropriately follow the Old Testament lesson.

Several metrical versions of the Magnificat are available in recent hymnals, as follows:

Baptist (1991), no. 81
Brethren and Mennonite (1992), no. 181; no. 703 is a prayer of confession based on the Magnificat.
Episcopal (1982), nos. 437-38
Lutheran (1978), no. 180
Presbyterian (1990): 600
Roman Catholic (*Worship,* 1986), no. 15
United Methodist (1989), nos. 198, 200

"Ye Who Claim the Faith of Jesus" (Episcopal, nos. 268-69; and United Methodist, no. 197) fits particularly well as the hymn at the reading of the Gospel lesson today. The first two stanzas might be used before the reading and the last two immediately after it.

Today's epistolary emphasis on the Incarnation ("a body you have prepared for me") calls to mind the following stanzas from John Henry Newman's great hymn "Praise to the Holiest in the Height."

O loving wisdom of our God!
When all was sin and shame,
a second Adam to the fight
and to the rescue came.

O wisest love! that flesh and blood,
which did in Adam fail,
should strive afresh against the foe,
should strive, and should prevail;

and that the highest gift of grace
should flesh and blood refine:
God's presence and his very self,
and essence all divine.

These lines could be used as a response to the epistle reading. Use the tune Christmas ("While Shepherds Watched Their Flocks").

The Gospel reading contains the lines that have been used in Marian devotion in the Western church for over a thousand years, "blessed are you among women and blessed is the fruit of your womb." The preacher may wish to call attention to the honor that the majority of Christians have paid to Mary over the centuries and help them explore why this has been so in terms of her devotion to the word of God which she heard and with which she cooperated. How does that make her a mother in faith and a model for all believing Christians? Various musical compositions based on the "Ave Maria" might be considered for use in today's service.

THE PASCHAL MYSTERY AND CHRISTMAS/EPIPHANY

Those who were trained in the old "pie chart" understanding of the Christian year may be a bit surprised to discover that the new calendar speaks of Christmas/Epiphany, with January 6 being the last day of Christmas, rather than the first day of a new season. The reason for this change is actually a return to the origins of both festivals, Christmas and Epiphany, and a recognition that the division of the two into separate seasons was really the result of Western chauvinism. Epiphany, the older of the two festivals, originated in the East, and celebrated both the birth and the baptism of Jesus. It also emphasized the mystery of the Incarnation as central to understanding these events. Christmas, as a feast of the nativity in particular, developed later in Rome. Some have maintained that December 25 was chosen to compete with the cult of Mithra, which celebrated the birth of its sun god on that day. Others suggest more complicated reasons having to do with dating back from what was believed to have been the date of the crucifixion.

December 25 won out in the Western church as the date for celebrating the birth of Jesus. Because January 6 had been so important earlier, it was retained, but the emphasis on Epiphany, the manifestation of God in the world, was reduced to the visit of the wise men, who were pictured as being of three races, so as to symbolize the whole world. The races were rarely ever pictured as including Caucasians, giving the impression that only "colored peoples" were in need of missionary outreach! In American Protestantism, this was to become the rationale for turning the season of Epiphany into a programmatic occasion emphasizing missions. Visiting missionaries combed the countrysides during the worst weather of the year in faithfulness to the pie chart, and confirmation classes were taught that green was the color of the season because it symbolized the growth of the church through missionary activity! The difficulty with this approach is not so much that it is misleading, but that it is so limited in its understanding of mission. The church's mission grows not out of the visit of the magi, but out of the whole work of Christ, and therefore mission is an appropriate topic at anytime, because it is the reason for the church's existence. The Western church's particular emphasis also led to an eclipse of the baptism of Jesus and it commemoration.

To counter some of this misunderstanding the new calendar observes a festival of the Incarnation and Manifestation from December 25 through January 6, Christmas through Epiphany. It then observes time "after Epiphany," or, in some traditions, "ordinary time." The First Sunday After Epiphany is the Baptism of the Lord, thus bringing that event into prominence once more.

Another difficulty with referring to the visit of the Magi as "the Epiphany" in such an exclusive way is that it ignores the fact that the Gospels are rich in epiphanies. The intent of the Gospels is to be an epiphany by recording "all that Jesus began to do and to teach." Having celebrated the birth of Jesus at Christmas/Epiphany, the time after Epiphany is spent examining who this is who has come among us. Each year the last Sunday after Epiphany, regardless of how many Sundays there may be, is the Sunday of the Transfiguration. This is the epiphany that begins the chain of events leading to Jesus' death and resurrection.

So it is the Paschal mystery that finally enables us to interpret Christmas and Epiphany. The Gospel writers constantly report the amazement or lack of comprehension that accompanies Jesus' ministry; understanding only comes by the light of the resurrection. As we do not celebrate Advent by pretending Christ has not come, so we do not celebrate Christmas by pretending we don't know what is going to happen to this child. Christmas cannot be celebrated properly in isolation from the rest of the Christ-event. To separate the story of Jesus' birth from the harsh reality of the crucifixion is to engage in a pious fraud, a sentimental blasphemy. Careful exegesis of the lessons for the time will make evident the opportunities the Scripture gives to relate incarnation and atonement, the cradle and the cross.

Because Epiphany day will usually fall during the week, the lectionary gives the option of substituting it and its lessons on the First Sunday After Christmas. Provided January 6 falls later than the Second Sunday After Christmas it could also be observed on that day. The reason for this is that the First Sunday After Epiphany is always the Baptism of the Lord, thus giving priority to an event that is attested to by all the Gospels. Because of space limitations, commentary on the Second Sunday After Christmas (whose propers never vary) may be found in the first volume of the Year A series.

The Services of Christmas

The Western Catholic tradition has observed three services for Christmas Day: one at midnight, one at dawn, and one during the day. That accounts for the three propers listed in the lectionary. Because of space, this series will deal with one proper each year. The lessons remain the same for all three years, and worship planners may exercise the option of changing the lessons around between the services. This is encouraged in the case of the Gospel reading for the service during the day, the Johannine prologue, if there is a chance that it will be omitted otherwise. For those who wish to use John 1 this year, see the exegetical comment in the first volume of the Year A series, where it also appears as the Gospel reading for the Second Sunday After Christmas.

The pattern in much of American Protestantism is to have one or two earlier services followed by a midnight service on Christmas Eve, and only in rare instances are services held on Christmas Day at all. Usually the earlier service is a "family" or "children's" service. The set of three propers in the lectionary can be adapted very easily to this tradition, particularly since the Gospel reading for the first two propers are the familiar Christmas story from Luke.

If there is a crèche in the church, the placing of the figure of Jesus in the manger might take place after the reading of Luke 2:7. This could be accompanied by the singing of one or more stanzas of "Away in a Manger," and the use of the following unison prayer:

> Lord Jesus,
> I offer to you
> the gold of my love,
> the incense of my prayers,
> the myrrh of my willingness to bear the cross.
> Amen.

The service would then continue with the reading of the Gospel. For those who object to such an interruption of the Gospel reading, this brief devotion can be used as an entrance rite at the beginning of the service, with the image of Jesus being brought in during the procession.

Christmas is a popular time for "candlelight services," and they are often advertised in such a way as to give the impression that the candlelight is an end in itself rather than a rich symbol of what the birth of Christ means to the world. Attention to the Paschal character of our worship will always help us guard against a manipulated sentimental religiosity. Ideally, the Advent wreath, with its function of "counting down" to Christmas, should disappear before the first service of the season. If it has come equipped with a "Christ candle," light only that candle for these services of Christmas Eve/Day. After that it should vanish, so as not to give the impression that it is on an equal footing with the Paschal candle, which is the primary light in the church symbolizing the presence of Christ. Again, it is the Paschal symbol that takes priority and gives meaning to what we are doing, even at Christmas.

Where the service involves all the members of the congregation having lighted candles, take care that directions are clear, brief, and to the point. The effect of the occasion is diminished if the pastor is giving warnings about dropping wax on the new carpet! Imaginative worship planners should think about how a service can be a "candlelight" service without having to put live flames in the hands of everyone present.

The midnight service is most appropriately eucharistic, and that emphasis should not be overshadowed by any candlelighting exercise, a case of bad liturgy driving out good. Christmas is the celebration of the Incarnation, the scandalous proclamation that God took on human flesh and blood. The elements of bread and wine remind us of this "materialistic" character of God who comes to meet us again in the Eucharist, a symbol of Christ incarnate.

Just as the services of Advent have been characterized by reserve and a sense of anticipation, so the services of Christmas unleash a torrent of praise and adoration through word, music, and visuals. Avoid clutter in both chancel and nave to allow for adequate liturgical movement. If live Christmas trees are used, let them be in proportion to the space, and, hopefully, potted, so that later they can be planted as a sign of ecological responsibility. Give some thought as to whether they are decorated or left bare. Candles and flowers should point to the Lord's Table, neither camouflaging it nor making it difficult to set for the Eucharist. The church's celebratory colors of white and/or gold are used during this time.

Christmas Day, Third Proper

Old Testament Texts

Isaiah 52:7-10 is a hymn of exultation celebrating the reign of God. Psalm 98 celebrates the enthronement of God in the Temple.

The Lesson: *Isaiah 52:7-10*

Does God Reign Everywhere?

Setting. The book of Isaiah is the prophetic voice of Zion traditions in the Old Testament. Zion is a belief system that rested on two fundamental convictions: (1) the primary conviction that God had chosen to dwell permanently in the Jerusalem Temple, and (2) a secondary belief that God had chosen to support the Davidic monarchy. Both of these beliefs are unconditional, which means that because no human action prompted God's decision to dwell with Israel in the first place, no human action could negate it. In other words, God is not free to break these promises under any conditions, hence they are secure for all of time. The heart of Zion traditions, therefore, concerns the presence of God, which gives rise to the use of the term *Immanuel* (God with us) in Isaiah (chapter 8), as well as hymns that celebrate the rule or kingship of God such as Psalm 98, the response for this Sunday. When interpreting Isaiah 52:7-10 the preacher can stress the point that the confession of divine presence in Zion is here not universal in scope. Immanuel is a confession about God in the Temple and perhaps by extension Jerusalem, but it is not a confession about God in Egypt, Moab, or any other place, including one's home outside of Jerusalem. Such a confession about the local presence of God gives rise to the distinction between the sacred (the place where God dwells) and the profane (the place where God does not dwell). Images of divine rule, therefore, are statements about God in a sacred place (the Jerusalem Temple) and not about God in

the countryside. This is not to deny that there are visions of God ruling universally in Zion tradition. These visions, however, are not presented as statements of fact, but as future goals. That God rules in
Jerusalem has implications for all persons, and one day the nations
will all make pilgrimages to Zion. This brief background allows us to
address the question that provides the heading to this commentary,
Does God reign everywhere? If one operates within the Zion tradition
the answer is, Certainly not! God reigns in the Jerusalem Temple.

First Isaiah (much of chapters 1–39) is the preexilic voice of Zion
tradition. A presupposition of this prophet was the fact that God rules
in the Temple. His call takes place in the Temple (Isaiah 6), and he
critically evaluates the king (Isaiah 7–9) and Israel (Isaiah 2–5) from
the perspective that he achieves by being in the presence of God
within the Temple. The Old Testament lesson for this Sunday is part
of the prophetic corpus attributed to exilic Second Isaiah, which at
the very least includes Isaiah 40–55. Second Isaiah is also a prophetic
voice within Zion tradition, but it is characterized by enormous innovation because of two problems: (1) the Temple and Jerusalem no
longer exist; (2) this prophet now finds himself in the profane world
of Babylon. These problems raise a series of theological questions
which include the following two: How do you confess the permanent
presence of God in the Temple when there isn't one? And is it possible to communicate with God without the Temple? The innovation of
Second Isaiah is that he explores how God can be active in the world
far beyond the walls of the Temple. The prophet achieves this goal
by exploring the creative power of God over all aspects of the creation (see the emphasis on creation in the closing part of the
prophet's call in 40:12-31). Furthermore, once God is let loose from
the Temple, God can call prophets and also save Israel even if they
are as far away as Babylon (see the opening part of the prophet's call
in 40:1-11). Does the fact that God can do all of these things—such
as influence the course of history, call prophets, and save Israel—
lead to the conclusion that God rules everywhere? The Old Testament lesson for this Sunday would answer the question, Certainly
not! The enthronement of God is still localized to the Temple. What
does this mean for preaching Isaiah 52:7-10 on Christmas?

Structure. Isaiah 52:7-10 is part of a larger section of literature that includes 51:9–52:10, which consists of a hymn (51:9–52:6), a narrative insertion (52:3-6), and a response to the hymn (52:7-10). This section begins with a wake-up call in 51:9. The Lord has been asleep and the hymn of 51:9–52:2 is an attempt to rouse God from slumber in order to enact a new exodus. The wake-up call is in two parts. First God is aroused from slumber (51:9), and then Zion is personified and also urged to wake up in preparation for a new salvation (52:1-2). A narrative section has been added to the hymn in 52:3-6 giving explicit commentary on the exile, before the lectionary text for this Sunday provides a response to the hymn in 51:9–52:6. The response in 52:7-10 picks up many of the images from the preexilic Jerusalem cult in order to describe the return of God to Jerusalem as a festival of enthronement.

Significance. Second Isaiah is an innovative voice in Zion tradition. Central to the prophet's message is that past tradition does not have the final word concerning the character of God's salvation. Thus God is the universal creator, who is able to call prophets in Babylon and even inaugurate a new exodus, but these radical insights do not lead to the conclusion that God is equally present in all places. The goal of a new exodus for Second Isaiah is Immanuel (God with the people of God); and, for this prophet, divine presence can only take place at God's official sanctuary. In spite of the innovative ways in which Second Isaiah begins to universalize God's power, consider how the prophet does not conclude that God is equally present in all places. The response to God's wake-up call is not a celebration of God's generalized presence with the people of God but an enthronement festival at a particular worship location. Isaiah 52:7 underscores how God reigns in Zion (not in Babylon). Verse 8 underscores how the guards will see the procession of God returning. Finally, vv. 9-10 personifies the city by describing how it will sing in response to God's return and how this enthronement could have universal implications.

When preaching Isaiah 52:7-10 on Christmas, we declare that the incarnation of God is rooted in Old Testament Zion tradition. It is the Christian version of celebrating Immanuel. Too often in contemporary reflection on Christmas we forget that incarnation is a confession of the presence of God within the worshiping community. It is not a generalized confession about the presence of God in all places. God rules as an infant in the midst of the people of God. This fact makes worship sacred. But what is true for the sacred is not necessarily true for the profane. Two implications for preaching follow from this. First, worship matters. It is the place where God is enthroned, rather than in our nation, in our local community, or even in our homes or individual selves. Second, once the distinction between the sacred and the profane is firmly established, then we can raise the question of what the enthronement of God in worship means for life outside of worship. This question creates tension, which gives rise to mission. What does it mean to live out one's life in daily routine when it is ruled in worship by an infant? How does such a confession of Immanuel provide a standard for critically evaluating our everyday notions of power, success, or even survival?

The Response: *Psalm 98*

A Celebration of God's Enthronement

Setting. Psalm 98 is a song of praise that celebrates the kingship of God in the Temple. This focus on God's rule and enthronement in the Temple is a theme also running through Psalms 47, 93, 96, 97, and 99.

Structure. Psalm 98 begins with an introit in v. 1*a*, before it separates into two parts, a recounting of God's power that has led to his victory and enthronement (vv. 1*b*-3) and an extended call to praise God (vv. 4-9).

Significance. Psalm 98 incorporates many of the motifs from Isaiah 52:7-10. The right hand of God as the source of victory occurs in Isaiah 52:10 and Psalm 98:1. Both texts also call for a breaking forth in song (Isaiah 52:9 and Psalm 98:4). The two passages underscore how God rules first in the context of the worshiping community and how this rule has potential significance in a universal context.

New Testament Texts

The readings are the opening sections of two of the books of the New Testament that are most elevated in style and most profound in

69

reflection. These beginning statements are especially polished, even poetic; and both are intensely focused on the person and work of Jesus Christ. Hebrews declares the superiority of Christ and John dwells on his incarnation, and both texts explain who he is and what he means for persons of faith.

The Epistle: *Hebrews 1:1-4 (5-12)*

Knowing God's Son

Setting. Commentators typically point out that Hebrews begins as a treatise, proceeds as a sermon, and ends as a letter; yet, the central sermonic materials that make up the bulk of the writing are cast with enigmatic philosophical questions that are not expected in most Christian preaching today. The document is a grand meditation on the superior character of the new Christian covenant, designed to undermine any nostalgia for the previous covenant that could motivate a return to former things. In its development Hebrews makes an intimate connection between theological argument and the interpretation of Scripture. In particular, this week's lesson comes from the introductory section of Hebrews (1:1–2:18). In this portion of the letter the author works with a collection of passages from the Old Testament about angels and argues concerning the superiority of Christ over the angels.

Structure. The verses that form our reading are the opening lines of the author's christocentric exposition. The first four verses are the formal introduction to the work, and they resound with the major theological themes of the complete composition. In these lines we encounter several structural elements. There is a contrast between "long ago" and "these last days," between "the prophets" and "a Son," and between "the Son" and "angels." In the course of making these contrasts, the author gives information about who God's Son is and what the Son has done (and is doing). The optional verses for this reading move past the act of opening to begin the author's deliberations, which are intended to demonstrate the unsurpassable superiority of Christ. These lines are in fact a pastiche of statements from the Old Testament, as is indicated by the manner in which the NRSV has set the text; they come from the Psalms, II Samuel, and Deuteronomy.

70

Significance. It is nearly impossible to exhaust the possibilities for proclamation in these verses. But, whatever tactic one takes in relation to this lesson, the overarching concern of the author that must inform any sermon is the magnitude of God's saving work in his Son, Jesus Christ, which surpasses all else that has gone before (and by implication, anything that follows).

The text begins by framing its proclamation in terms of God's time. God has worked in the past in a variety of ways, and the author singles out the prophets for special mention—perhaps because of the relationship between their work and preaching and what the author contends God accomplished in Jesus Christ. Yet, now God has gone beyond all that went before by speaking to humanity through his Son. We learn that this Son is "heir to all things"—that is, he has been named master of all God's creation, and this is especially fitting because it is through this Son that God created all that God brought into existence. The beauty of this scheme is its sense of continuity and completion. The one through whom God gave creation its beginning is now established as the one to whom all creation belongs. Thus, the Son is both creator and Lord.

In turn, we learn more about (1) who the Son is, (2) what he has done and is doing, and (3) what that means. First, the Son is "the reflection of God's glory and the exact imprint of God's very being." Second, he has "made purification for sins" and he "sustains all things by his powerful word" as he sits "at the right hand of the Majesty on high." Third, this means in his person and work he is "much superior to angels." Seeing the point these lines make is helpful, but each of these phrases (and others in the text) are theologically loaded, and careful consultation of a serious scholarly commentary is practically required. In brief, however, these phrases articulate a high Christology that asserts the divinity, preexistence, (Incarnation, not explicit here), exaltation, and rule of the Son. The author believes the Son created, redeemed, and rules the world. Indeed the world had its beginning and now is sustained by God's power at work through the Son.

One may sincerely wonder how the author knows all that he tells us in these verses. In the following collection of lines from the Old Testament, we see something of the manner in which this author and the early Christian community gained ever deepening understanding of the person and the work of Jesus Christ. They read Scripture—in light of their experience of Jesus and in light of their faith in his saving death and resurrection—to learn more about their Lord. This is not modern historical-critical exegesis, nor is it mere prooftexting; rather, this is a hermeneutically sophisticated method of textual interpretation that shows us at least two things: (1) The early Christians had a high regard for the authority and message of Scripture, and (2) the engagement with Scripture was understood as penultimate in nature, following from a vital faith in a living Lord to whom the early believers understood themselves to be dynamically related.

The Gospel: *John 1:1-9 (10-18)*

The Word in the World

Setting. These opening verses of the gospel according to John are often called the prologue to the Gospel, for they function as a kind of frontispiece to the writing. In quasi-poetic fashion these lines declare themes that give the readers of John a profoundly theological perspective on the story, the teachings, and the truth-claims that follow.

Structure. The prologue is formed, as is the rest of the Gospel, by a rich, complex combination of historical memory, poetic expression about the person and work of Jesus Christ, and narrative commentary. The alternation between styles of writing, points of view, and types of reflection should provide much inspiration for those designing both preaching and worship.

One may cluster and contemplate the statements in these verses in terms of point of view: poetic confession comes in vv. 1-5, 10-12*a*, 14, 16; vv. 6-7, 15 are historical reporting about John the Baptist; and narrative commentary, frequently with a confessional bent, occurs in vv. 8-9, 12*b*-13, 17-18. Viewed in another manner, one may evaluate the passage in terms of its poetic (vv. 1-5, 10-12*a*, 14, 16) or prose (vv. 6-9, 12*b*-13, 15, 17-18) style.

Significance. There is no way to treat all aspects of this passage adequately in a brief space, so that one is tempted to omit treating the "optional" lines. But the manner in which vv. 1-18 cohere makes it necessary to deal with the larger reading. Verses 1-2 open with words similar to the creation story in Genesis 1. The idea at the heart of these lines is that the Word was with God in heaven before creation. Verses 3-5 recall the act of creation through the Word-present-with-God and emphasize the Word's role as sustainer; but then the text mentions darkness, a poetic allusion to the Fall, and alters the Word metaphor for Jesus Christ into the metaphor of Light, a poetic allusion to Jesus Christ's work as Redeemer. Verses 6-9 interrupt the poetry and move the mind of the reader into the recent past world of Palestine, mentioning John the Baptist and his limited role as prophetic witness to the coming Light (perhaps articulating a polemic against followers of the Baptist who made messianic claims about him). Verses 10-12a speak of the coming of the Word into the world as a past event, of his rejection by "his own people" (perhaps a reference to non-Christian Jews; but since the Word made all humans the phrase may be a broader reference); and the lines speak finally about the Word's redeeming effect on the lives of believers. Verses 12b-13 explain that the empowerment of believers to be God's children is the work of God alone. Verse 14 meditates on the Incarnation, the historical interaction of believers with the Word-made-flesh, and the believers perception of the glory of "the Son" who was filled with God's eternal love. Verse 15 underlines the validity of the christological claims advanced in the passage by citing the testimony of John the Baptist. Then, v. 16 speaks of the believers sharing in the love of the Word-become-flesh; this is a kind of poetic explanation of the existential dimensions of redemption. Finally, v. 17 explains in historical terms the statement of v. 16, drawing a comparison of law and love, of Moses and Jesus Christ (not so much to denounce Moses as to emphasize the superiority of Jesus Christ); and v. 18 boldly declares that the Son of God, Jesus Christ, has revealed the unseen Father to humankind.

The heart of this magnificent passage is christological. Jesus Christ, the Son of God, is God's eternal Word, and as such he is Creator, Redeemer, and Revealer. All his work is characterized by love. From this passage we can contemplate the work of Christ and come to comprehend that all God's dealings with humanity are motivated by God's love. God is love, as John's Gospel tells us. Life

73

is given, sustained, and redeemed because of and through God's love. And, how do we know it? Because unseen God has been revealed in Jesus Christ. The Word came into the world as an act of divine love, in order to incorporate an all too unlovely humanity into the primary experience of God's love.

Christmas Day: The Celebration

There are three sets of lessons (propers) appointed for Christmas Day, and they remain the same all three years. For reasons of space, Proper 1 was discussed in Year A and Proper 2 in Year B. Now we shall consider Proper 3.

Three sets are appointed because of the tradition in the Western church of celebrating Mass (the Christ-mass) three times on Christmas Day. The first Mass was at midnight, the second at dawn, and the third during the day. The Gospel readings for the first two Masses are from the Lukan birth narratives. Proper 3 concerns itself with the theological implications of those stories as reflected in Hebrews and John.

An article in a national newspaper recently spoke of the stress that Jews undergo during the celebration of Christmas in this primarily Christian culture. It spoke of the subtle and nonverbal pressures throughout the community to force some kind of celebrative conformity that has resulted in the popularization of Hanukkah, replete with candles, gift-giving, and Hanukkah bushes. The author deplored the exaltation of Hanukkah as being subversive of the Passover as the primary festival that forms and locates Jewish identity, and attributed it to the desire to have at the same time as their neighbors a festival that sums up the meaning of their religious faith. It is ironic that the author little appreciated that the problem is precisely the same for Christians! When Christmas is seen as the primary celebrative expression of Christian faith, we have lost the essential source of our identity, the Paschal mystery. Even the celebration of Epiphany historically preceded the celebration of Christmas. It is for this reason that these lessons appear today, to root us theologically and to help us understand Christmas precisely as a commentary on Easter.

Because it is so important to connect Christmas to Easter, the longer form of the Gospel reading is to be preferred. Verses 1-9 are sufficient to provide scriptural warrant for a cozy candlelighting service, but vv. 10-18 are absolutely necessary if the scandal of the Incarnation is to be proclaimed. "The Word was made flesh" provides the theological locus for the preaching of the Incarnation and its sacramental recalling in the celebration of the Holy Eucharist. To Christian ears, the Old Testament lesson will be a reminder of the localized presence of Christ in the Lord's Supper, a presence that is unconditional (see Old Testament commentary above) and in no way depends upon our goodness or merit or even degree of faith. So it may be said of us as of others of old, "he came to what was his own, and his own people did not accept him." For a congregation saturated with the saccharin of the season, this can be a time to provide a healthy theological antidote by talking about the "scandal of particularity," how God chooses and uses the most unlikely people, places, and things to come to us in spite of us. And for Christians, that scandal has to do particularly with Jesus of Nazareth and with things like water and bread and wine.

Note that "Joy to the World" is a paraphrase of vv. 4-9 of Psalm 98, and so would serve as today's response to the Old Testament lesson.

First Sunday After Christmas

Old Testament Texts

I Samuel 2:18-20, 26 is an account of Samuel's service as a boy at the Shiloh cult and Eli's blessing of Hannah for giving Samuel back to God. Psalm 148 is a hymn of praise.

The Lesson: *I Samuel 2:18-20, 26*

Samuel at Shiloh

Setting. The Old Testament lesson about Samuel's service to God at the Shiloh cult must be read in the larger context of Hannah's barrenness, which was the central motif in I Samuel 1:1–2:10. The location for action in these opening chapters is the Shiloh cult. The book opens in 1:3 by noting how Elkanah would make a yearly pilgrimage to Shiloh for worship and sacrifice. The first scene of the story pictures Hannah at the Shiloh cult making a vow to God (1:11) that if she were given a son, she would give him back to God. The second scene takes place a year later, when Hannah brings her new born baby to the Shiloh cult in order to fulfill her vow (1:21-28). This scene ends with her song of praise in 2:1-10. The lesson for this Sunday begins to shift the focus from Hannah to Samuel and how he served God in the Shiloh cult. Yet the structure of yearly visits to the Shiloh cult by the family of Elkanah is maintained, and, because of this, the character of Hannah still retains a role in the story (see 2:18-19 and 21).

Structure. The lectionary reading is part of a larger structure that includes I Samuel 2:11–4:1*a*. This section is organized in such a way that reports concerning the evil character of Eli's sons are contrasted with descriptions about the integrity of Samuel already as a young boy. First Samuel 2:11 begins by noting how Samuel remained at the Shiloh cult to serve God when his family returned home to Ramah. First Samuel 2:12-17 shifts the focus from Samuel to Hophni and Phinehas to underscore how they abused their priestly office. First Samuel 2:20-21 turns our attention back to Samuel and Hannah momentarily where the scene becomes idyllic once again— Hannah is pictured bringing Samuel priestly robes on yearly visits, Eli is present bestowing priestly blessings, and Hannah is having more children, while Samuel continues to serve God. Then a shift occurs again in I Samuel 2:22-25 where the conflict between Eli and his sons over the abuse of priestly responsibility takes center stage, before it is interrupted for one verse (v. 26), which reminds the reader of how Samuel was in fact growing in his maturity as a priestly figure. These conflicting portraits of activity at the Shiloh cult set the stage for the prophetic condemnation of the house of Eli by the man of God in vv. 27-36, which is followed by the call of Samuel in 3:1–4:1a. This overview of I Samuel 2:11–4:1a shows how the lectionary reading consists of two distinct portraits of Samuel (2:18-20, 26) that have now been taken out of their context where their function was to provide contrast with Eli's family.

Significance. The Old Testament lesson can be approached in two ways for preaching. One way is to interpret the text in conjunction with the New Testament lesson. There are clear indications that Luke has used the early chapters of I Samuel to construct the birth and infancy narratives of Jesus in his Gospel. There are close parallels, for example, between Hannah's song in I Samuel 2:1-10 and the Magnificat in Luke 1:46-55. The limitation of the Old Testament lesson to the portraits of Samuel growing up in the Shiloh temple invites further comparison to Luke 2:41-52 where Jesus is also pictured as needing to "be in [his] Father's house" (1:49). One aspect of I Samuel 2:18-20, 26 stands out in particular when the text is read interbiblically—namely, the importance of the temple as the location for divine activity. Both stories underscore how God is present in a special way in the setting of worship.

First Samuel 2:18-20, 26 can also be interpreted independently from the Gospel lesson, but in this case the preacher may wish to expand the boundaries of the text for two reasons. First, the structure has underscored how important the contrast is between Samuel and

77

Eli's sons. A second reason for expanding the boundaries of the text is that Hannah is still an important character in the Old Testament lesson, and her story requires the addition of v. 21. In fact, one could argue that she is more central to I Samuel 2:18-20 than her son. Verse 19 describes how she visited Samuel yearly at the Shiloh cult center. Verse 20 consists of a blessing to her for having fulfilled her vow by giving Samuel to Eli. Finally, v. 21, underscores how God took note of her faithfulness. The important role of Hannah in her yearly visits to Samuel, as well as the contrast between Samuel and the house of Eli, illustrate how the divine choice of Samuel to replace the house of Eli is taking place in a larger network of human actions. This network includes the morally strong Hannah over against the morally evil Hophni and Phinehas with the more ambiguous Eli in the middle. This text provides an occasion for the preacher to explore the activity of God in larger community structures that are often a mixture of good and bad characters. The story illustrates how divine blessing and judgment take on form in conjunction with human action.

The Response: *Psalm 148*

A Hymn of Praise

Setting. Psalm 148 is probably best categorized as a hymn of praise in which imperative forms of the verb *praise* predominate (note the repetition of the imperative, Praise! or Let them praise! in vv. 1, 2, 3, 4, 5, 7, 13, 14). The scope of the psalm is so wide in its call to praise that all aspects of creation are included. This larger vision gives rise to a second characteristic of this hymn, which is the strong presence of wisdom motifs, especially evident in the listing of different elements in nature, which are called upon to praise God.

Structure. The psalm separates into two parts, vv. 1-6 and 7-14. Verses 1-6 are a call to praise God from heaven, while vv. 7-14 repeat the command but this time from the earth. Each of these sections further separates into three parts: (1) Each section begins with a command to praise (from heaven, vv. 1-4 and from earth, vv. 7-12). (2) The command is followed in each case with a summary statement, which includes a reason why God should be praised (vv. 5 and 13). These sections are signaled in each case through the repetition of the phrase, "Let them praise the name of the Lord" (vv. 5*a* and 13*a*). The reason for praise from the hosts of heaven is that God created them (v. 5*b*), while earthly creatures must praise God because only the Lord is exalted on earth (v. 13*b*). (3) Finally, each section ends with a summary statement about God (vv. 6 and 14) in relationship to the hosts of heaven and earth (specifically Israel).

Significance. When Psalm 148 is read as a response to I Samuel 2:18-20 (21), 26 it becomes an extension of Hannah's praise that was begun in her first hymn (2:1-10). Its use in the liturgy provides an opportunity for the worshiping community to identify with the portrait of Hannah and Samuel over against Eli's sons.

New Testament Texts

The readings focus on the meaning of Christ for Christian life and the person of Christ in the context of history. They complement one another more than they work in tandem, though for issuing and answering a call to Christ-likeness (Colossians) it is important to understand the Christ who is the focus of conversation (Luke).

The Epistle: *Colossians 3:12-17*

Living Through the Lord Jesus Christ

Setting. In geographical terms Colossae was the least significant city to which one of the thirteen canonical letters attributed to Paul was written. In the mid-first century this former city had declined into a small town, which was destroyed by an earthquake in 63 C.E. and apparently never rebuilt. The letter itself indicates that the Colossians were enamored or were in danger of being enamored of a strange syncretistic religio-philosophy based on wisdom speculation. Colossians 2:8 refers to the "philosophy" and 2:23 makes clear the ascetic tendency of the thought and practice. In turn, 2:18 shows that somehow, someone thought and taught that through self-abasement the Colossians could experience "the worship of the angels"—most likely meaning "to join the angels in worship." Moreover, the practice of achieving ecstasy through self-denial had been mixed with the teachings of Christianity. The letter seeks to correct and to clarify the situation.

Colossians combines large sections of theological and ethical instruction. At times one wonders whether a statement is doctrinal or practical, or both. This reading comes at the end of the portion of the letter scholars understand to be the "body" of the letter (1:9–3:17)— that is, the more doctrinal section. There is, however, a hortatory quality to these verses, though upon study one finds the material more abstract than the pointed parenetic material that follows in 3:18–4:6.

Structure. Colossians 3:1-17 is a recognizable unit within the doctrinally oriented portion of the letter. In 3:1-4 the readers are told that since they have been raised with Christ they are to seek heavenly ways. Verses 5-17 work out the meaning of this teaching: First, vv. 5-11 instruct believers to put away ("put to death") impurity ("what is earthly"); second, vv. 12-17 direct them to put on what is "of" Christ, which generates a life of loving thankfulness to God. The manner of speaking shifts through these verses from (1) putting on heavenly things to (2) living according to the model of the Lord to (3) love above all to (4) the peace of Christ and the word of Christ to (5) doing all in the name of the Lord Jesus, which means thanks to God through him.

Significance. It is crucial for preaching to notice that the Greek text signals the relative nature of the instruction given here with the word *therefore* at the outset of v. 12. The same was the case at v. 5, so that the directions here depend upon and extend from the thought of 3:1-4. The Colossians have died to the ways of the world and been raised with Christ who is their very life! They are called to put on the things of Christ because they are in Christ and he is in them giving them new life.

In the context of the Christmas season we can understand that God's gift to us of Jesus Christ means that our lives have changed and are being changed. The life we are called to live is realized by the life of Christ which has been given to us for our transformation. The strong call to a Christ-like life is possible because the life of Christ is real, and it takes hold of our lives and directs them toward godliness. These verses are much more than mere moral advice cast in theological terms. We find here a declaration out of the depth of faith's perception of the wonderful operation of God's grace.

When we hear that "as the Lord has forgiven you [plural], so you also must forgive" we should understand "because the Lord has forgiven us, thus we are able and must forgive each other." Far more than simply stating a new standard, this line articulates the profound theological truth of the new life achieved by God's love at work through Jesus Christ. The gift of Christ is the gift of a new context ("the body of Christ") and a new power ("love") for living. Moreover, the message of Christ ("the word of Christ") is given to us as a new focal point directing our lives toward God. Finally, v. 17 declares the all-encompassing, all-transforming character of the gift of our lives lived in relation to Christ. The characteristic of such life is genuine gratitude toward God.

The Gospel: *Luke 2:41-52*

Jesus Who Amazed

Setting. The first two chapters of Luke focus on the time before the appearance of the adult Jesus in ministry. In general the materials in Luke 1–2 are a series of memorable stories and reports, which work out a comparison between John the Baptist and Jesus by focusing on the annunciations of their births, the births per se, their circumcisions, their being named, and prophetic declarations that were made concerning them. The conclusion of the material about John comes in Luke 1:80 when Luke simply reports that the child John grew and became strong in the Spirit and was in the wilderness until the time when he appeared preaching. The story told in this week's lesson is the final portion of material concerning Jesus' early life. Noticeably the story told here of the incident in the Temple, when Jesus was twelve, ends with a statement (v. 52) that is similar to the concluding lines of the Baptist material.

Structure. The lesson is essentially a sequential narrative with reports of direct statements and a sweeping narrative summary in conclusion. Verses 41-42 set the context of family piety and pilgrimage, in which vv. 43-45 tell of Jesus' independent behavior and explains how Mary and Joseph did not know of Jesus' whereabouts. The narrative takes on sharper focus in vv. 46-50, as Luke describes the amazing situation that the parents eventually discovered—

namely, the boy Jesus sitting in the Temple among the teachers engaging in conversation that astonished all who heard his questions and answers. Luke records a strange conversation between Mary and Jesus and goes on to recognize the lack of understanding within the parents. And in these verses the pronouncement by the boy Jesus in v. 49 dominates. Finally, Luke summarizes the situation and the future development of Jesus in v. 52. Though the story line is clear, unraveling the pieces is challenging.

Significance. Many sermons have boiled these verses down to pious pabulum by focusing on Jesus' spiritual formation in the context of family devotion. Thus, one gets a generic sermon on "growing children unto God" that advocates family piety. Others have abused the text by turning the reference to the boy Jesus' understanding into a denunciation of Judaism. The story is striking, but it is also difficult to reckon with for preaching. Yet, inherent in the whole story are important clues for interpretation and use in proclamation.

The ending Luke offers in v. 52 signals the major concern of the previous account. Therefore, this story is neither a narrative primarily concerned with general spiritual formation nor an account treating sociological issues. Rather, Luke dramatically draws our attention to a crucial christological point: Jesus, God's Son, possessed amazing wisdom, and one learns through this account that the essence of his wisdom, the heart of his godly life, was his attending to God's own concerns. One should notice, however, that this simple point is neither small nor smooth, for Jesus' behavior baffled his parents as much as his questions and answers amazed his hearers.

One other striking dimension of this story stimulates the homiletical imagination. Luke tells us that Mary and Joseph located Jesus after three days. Whether this temporal note means they found him three days after they missed him or three days after they came back to Jerusalem is finally impossible to determine. But, despite the context and the ill-fit, few Christians can hear these words without thinking ahead to the Resurrection. Indeed, in focusing on the "childhood" story we may never forget that the boy in this story grew up to be the man who preached the kingdom of God, died on the cross, and was raised from the dead. We celebrate Christmas because of the reality of Holy Week, so that as we ponder the Christmas gift of God's own Son we must recall both the price of that gift and the faithful power of God, which gives saving meaning to Jesus' life and work.

Christmas 1: The Celebration

It should be remembered in preparing the service for this day that the Church is still involved in the celebration of the Christmas mystery, the mystery of the Incarnation. Just as the secular culture is overly anxious to begin the celebration of Christmas, so it is now impatient to get the tree to the curbside, the pine needles vacuumed up, the presents put away, and the Christmas compact discs stored away until Thanksgiving. To this haste to leave the manger, the Church replies by keeping the tree and poinsettias on display and continuing to sing carols and other Christmas music.

The theme of family is evident in the Old Testament and Gospel readings, but the epistle reading makes clear that the family of interest today is the family that is the Church of Jesus Christ. Nuclear families are informed by what it means to participate in the community of the baptized, so any preaching about "family values" ought to take seriously the radical ethic of Jesus as portrayed in today's epistle and in Luke's Gospel, which is the controlling Gospel for Year C. (See Janet Fishburn's account in *Confronting the Idolatry of Family*, Abingdon Press, 1991.) Intercessions for this Sunday may appropriately include prayers for families, for programs of religious education, and for children around the world.

The epistle may be used selectively to provide introductions to the various parts of the liturgy, as follows:

CALL TO WORSHIP

With gratitude in your hearts sing psalms, hymns, and spiritual songs to God.

CALL TO CONFESSION

Let us confess our sins before the Lord, seeking both God's forgiveness and the grace to forgive one another.

PRAYER BEFORE SCRIPTURE

Grant, O God, the word of Christ to dwell in us richly, so that, being clothed in love, which binds everything together in perfect harmony, we may teach and admonish one another in all wisdom; through Christ the Light. Amen.

PRAYERS OF PETITION

A suitable collect may be composed to accompany each of the following invitations or silence may be kept with a single concluding collect at the end:

> Let us pray for the gift of compassion.
> Let us pray for an increase in kindness toward others.
> Let us pray for a share in the humility of Jesus.
> Let us pray for that meekness which puts others first.
> Let us pray for patience in our daily relationships.

DISMISSAL

Let the peace of Christ rule in your hearts, to which you were called in the one body; and whatever you do, in word or deed, do everything in the name of the Lord Jesus.

Preachers may wish to call attention to the chain of virtues in v. 12 of the epistle, since these are not an indiscriminate list of behaviors that Paul thought would "be nice," but they are linked together in a necessary fashion. Compassion, the ability to participate in another's pain and suffering, is productive of kindness, the desire to do something to assuage that pain. Kindness calls for humility, otherwise we become proud of our good works, and we look upon those to whom we minister as somehow less than we. Humility involves meekness (or, in French, the ability to be *débonnaire*), because humility is often misunderstood by those who live with other values, and meekness helps us accept that misunderstanding with equanimity rather than getting ourselves all worked up into a fit of self-justification. And finally, patience brings us back to compassion, because both are based on the same word, but now the patience is what is needed to endure suffering in our own right (probably because we have exercised kindness, etc.!). How's that for a catalog of family values?

84

New Year's Day

Old Testament Texts

Ecclesiastes 3:1-13 is the familiar poem about appointed times and seasons. Psalm 8 is a hymn that celebrates the creative power of God.

The Lesson: *Ecclesiastes 3:1-13*

Living Within Limits

Setting. The title of Ecclesiastes in Hebrew is *Qoheleth,* which means preacher. Scholars characterize the book as skeptical wisdom. This means at the very least that it is literature critical of the assumptions of classical wisdom (like Proverbs), which represented a certain confidence in the human ability to know God, to act in accordance with the divine will, and to profit from such knowledge both spiritually and socially in this life. Scholars agree that skeptical wisdom raises fundamental questions about whether God's motives and actions could be known by humans. But there is debate among scholars concerning how skeptical *Qoheleth* may be. The debate can be encapsulated by looking briefly at the rather ambiguous term *hebel* in Hebrew, which plays a central role in Qoheleth. The book opens with the bold statement in 1:2: *hebel habalim 'amar qohelet, habel habalim hakkol habel.* Note how the word *hebel* is used no less than five times. The NRSV translates this verse: "Vanity of vanities, says the Teacher, vanity of vanities! All is vanity." The translation suggests that the preacher is making a strong value statement about the worthlessness or futility of life ("Life is vain"). From this point of view one could conclude that the central message of *Qoheleth* is one of despair. God is unknowable and even ominous to humans, while human life evinces no clear patterns, and what is sure

85

in the end is that death cancels everything. See the *Old Testament Library Commentary* by J. L. Crenshaw for an interpretation of *Qoheleth* that moves along these lines. But the Hebrew word *hebel* can also take on the meaning of impermanence, such as breath. R. B. Y. Scott illustrates the meaning of impermanence when he translates *hebel* in his *Anchor Bible Commentary on Ecclesiastes*: "A vapor of vapors! (says *Qoheleth*). Thinnest of vapors. All is vapor!" The meaning that arises from this translation is not so much that human life is worthless, but that it is characterized by limitations ("Life is fleeting"). From this point of view the central message of *Qoheleth* is that humans are not gods; thus, in contrast to the claim of classical wisdom, humans can neither understand divine motive nor predict divine actions. The reader of *Qoheleth* must move with caution because both meanings will occur throughout the book. Is the ambiguity also true for 3:1-13? Is the lectionary text about the meaningless of human life before an ominous God, or about the limitation of human life in relationship to God—which, when understood, can lead to wisdom and fear of God? The present interpretation will argue for the latter reading.

Structure. Chapter 3 separates into four parts. It begins with the poem in vv. 1-8, which is introduced in v. 1 with a statement about times and season before 14 antitheses are listed (a time to be born and a time to die, . . . a time for war, and a time for peace). The next two sections (vv. 9-14 and 15-22) provide the preacher's response to the fact of appointed times and seasons. Each of these sections begins with the interrogative Hebrew pronoun *mah* (v. 9 introduces a question, "What gain have the workers from there toil?" while in v. 15 the pronoun introduces a statement of fact, "That which is, already has been; that which is to be, already is; and God seeks out what has gone by [or perhaps better, what is pursued]"). Then each opening statement is followed by the preacher describing what he has seen—Hebrew, *ra'ah* (in v. 10 the preacher sees the business of humanity and in v. 16 he sees that wickedness has replaced justice and righteousness). The perception of the preacher leads to statements about knowledge or the lack of it—Hebrew, *yada'* (in vv. 12, 14, and 21). Finally the chapter ends with the preacher making a concluding statement in v. 22 about what he has seen—Hebrew, *ra'ah*. The chapter can be outlined in the following manner.

I. The poem about set times and seasons (vv. 1-8)
II. The first response by the preacher about human limitations (vv. 9-14)
  A. What (*mah*) gain have the workers from their toil? (v. 9)
  B. I saw (*ra'ah*) (vv. 10-11)
  C. I know (*yada'*) (v. 12)
  D. I know (*yada'*) (v. 14)
III. The second response by the preacher about righteousness and justice (vv. 15-21)
  A. That (*mah*) which is. . . . (v. 15)
  B. I saw (*ra'ah*) (v. 16)
  C. I said in my heart (vv. 17-20)
  D. Who knows (*yada'*) (v. 21)
IV. A concluding summary—I saw (*ra'ah*) (v. 22)

The outline illustrates how the boundaries of the lectionary must be adjusted to include either vv. 1-14 or the entire chapter. In either case vv. 1-13 do not constitute a unit within the book.

Significance. Chapter 3 is not a soliloquy about the meaninglessness of human life. Rather it is a statement about the vast difference between God and humans, and the folly of human action that ignores this fact. The text provides a strong contemporary statement about the folly of frenetic activity for its own sake. The opening poem in vv. 1-8 sets the stage for the discussion of the preacher by establishing the fact that life adheres to set rhythms. The preacher makes two arguments in vv. 9-14 and 15-21.

The first speech (vv. 9-14) raises the question of whether life is meaningful, if, in fact, all times and seasons are preestablished (v. 9). The question forces an answer because we humans, the preacher notes, do have a sense of past and future, and this gives rise to the desire either to predict the different times of our lives, or, even better, to control them (v. 11*a*). Such action is futile, according to the preacher, because we cannot know divine motive (v. 11*b*). Instead wisdom consists of two conclusions offered by the preacher: (1) that human life should be enjoyed within the rhythm established by God rather than in an attempt to change it; and, (2) that God should be feared (or perhaps better revered) because he is the one who has determined the cycles of life.

The second speech (vv. 15-21) moves more explicitly to the subject of human ethics. This speech begins in v. 15 with the two-part statement (1) that God has set the structures and boundaries of life and (2) that God seeks out or observes actions that take place within these set boundaries (translating the Hebrew *nirdap* as "what is pursued" rather than the NRSV "what has gone by"). The preacher sees that wickedness has replaced justice, and concludes that God will judge accordingly. The text ends in v. 22 by repeating the conclusion of the first speech, that humans should live life to the fullest within the set structures determined by God.

For *Qoheleth*, one human life is little more than a blip on God's radar screen. But even that blip is evaluated critically by God with the criteria of justice and righteousness. In view of this situation, wisdom for *Qoheleth* (which we defined early as the quest to know God, to act in accordance with the divine will, and to profit from such knowledge both spiritually and socially in this life) would mean that humans know their limitations and live within them, rather than trying to change them through frenetic activity.

The Response: *Psalm 8*

What Are Humans?

Setting. Psalm 8 is a hymn of praise, which modulates between an individual voice (vv. 1b-8) and a community refrain (vv. 1a, 9). The central motif of the community refrain is the celebration of the name of God.

Structure. Psalm 8 separates into two sections: vv. 1-4 and 5-9. The community refrain begins the first section (v. 1a) and concludes the last section (v. 9), with the result that the praise of God's name throughout the earth frames the entire psalm. The voice of the individual singer takes up the middle portion of the psalm. Within this section, the central theme of the psalm appears to be the question of v. 4: "What are human beings that you are mindful of them?" Most commentators agree that this question and the description of the role of humans in creation that follows in vv. 6-8 is based on the account of creation of humans in Genesis 1:26. Thus Psalm 8 should be read as interbiblical reflection on Genesis 1.

Significance. Psalm 8 is somewhat unusual in that it is a hymn of praise that addresses God in the second person ("you"). The use of the second person establishes a certain intimacy in the relationship between singer and God, which is striking because it contrasts with the vast (and impersonal) creation imagery that is the subject matter of much of the hymn (God is sovereign, majestic, creator of heavens, moon and stars, etc.). This contrast between the intimate relationship of singer and God, on the one hand, and the vastness of the creation order, on the other, is an important point of entry into interpreting Psalm 8, for it provides the background for the central question in v. 4. What are humans to God in the larger context of the universe? On such a large stage our first response would be that humans are insignificant to the larger drama of creation. Psalm 8 is a hymn of praise because exactly the opposite is true. God is not only mindful of earthbound mortals (v. 4), but he has even given them a formative role as actors on the large stage of creation. One suspects that this paradox (between the insignificance of humans in the larger order of creation and the degree of attention that God bestows on them) may provide insight for interpreting v. 2, which has no parallel any place in Scripture. Perhaps it is the frail human mortals who are the babes of v. 2 that God has chosen as a defense against evil ("Out of the mouths of babes and infants you have founded a bulwark . . . "), even though God had so many more resources at his disposal (see v. 1*b*, "You have set your glory above the heavens."). This fact is then what prompts the wonder and awe of the psalmist concerning the position of humans in the larger drama of God's creation. When the psalm is read as a response to Ecclesiastes 3 it reinforces the interpretation followed above: human life may be limited, but it is not worthless.

New Testament Texts

These lessons about "the end" speak of the glory of God's future and issue powerful proclamations of good news. The verses from Revelation are fully concerned with the future, though as a message about the ultimate revelation and accomplishments of God's glory at the end they are certainly meant to inspire hope for life before the end. The lesson from Matthew deals directly with the end of time as we know it, and the dramatic lines inspire awe as they tell of God's promised judgment at the end. As we look toward the new year, these readings help us focus on the future from a particularly Christian perspective.

The Epistle: *Revelation 21:1-6a*

Seeing the End and Knowing What It Means

Setting. The book of Revelation is a remarkable early Christian writing. It forms a fitting final document for the New Testament (and the Bible), for it testifies to that which is anticipated in all that went before—namely, the ultimate triumph of God. The work comprises three literary types. Dominantly, Revelation is a piece of apocalyptic literature, but worked into this kind of writing are epistles (chapters 2 and 3) and several prophetic declarations (part of our lesson). Discerning the style in which a section is written assists greatly in interpreting the various parts of the whole.

The general segment of the book from which our lesson comes is a great vision of the end that is recorded in 19:1–22:5. More specifically, our text is part of the vision of the new Jerusalem and the final word of God, 21:1-8. This is the last vision in a series of visions reported throughout the larger section.

Structure. These six verses are loaded! First, John of Patmos, the seer of Revelation, beholds the new heaven and the new earth. Second, he observes the descent of the new Jerusalem. Third, as John watches, a voice from the throne interprets the twin vision by declaring the nature of the new relationship established between God and humans at the end. And, fourth, "the one who was seated on the throne" gives John a command to write, and then, (fifth?) that same figure (God) declares the completion of the divine work of redemption.

Significance. The vision is actually a double vision, telling of the same divine work in two ways (vv. 1-2). The voice explains the meaning of the events (vv. 3-4) and the truth of the vision and its explanation are confirmed explicitly by God (vv. 5-6a).

The reporting of a vision is typical of apocalyptic literature, though plainly a prophetic declaration is reported in the course of John's telling of the vision. Apocalyptic literature is akin to prophetic literature in that both probe the end or future of human history, but it seems to come from a situation of persecution and to be directed to people who are ostracized in order to offer them an encoded word of bold assurance. The visions reported prior to this one are primarily negative, but this final vision is purely positive.

God's triumph that is promised at the end is nothing other than the completion of God's work of redemption. Yet, we should be careful to notice that redemption is not a way forward into the past, as if by forging ahead God could or would take us back to the Garden of Eden. Redemption establishes something that goes beyond all that went before. Even in the Garden when God walked with humans, God's home was not with them. Thus, current creation theologies celebrate a goodness that is inadequate by the standards of the book of Revelation. The end toward which God is moving is not a mere renewal of the present creation (as the Hebrew prophetic tradition would have it), rather God brings forth a new cosmological context in which a new city exists that is home to both God and humanity.

The images of the vision and the words from the throne seek to speak of that which is unspeakable. What God promises is far more than a qualitatively advanced existence similar to the lives we now live. In the new creation there is no chaos, death, or despair; but life with God means more than the elimination of these negative elements of our current lives. Yet, even through vision and divine declaration John can only tell of the new promised home of God and humanity by pointing out what will not be there rather than by telling of what is there (other than God and humans). The glories of the promised triumph go beyond the words and images whereby we may comprehend. Yet, the truth of the promise is confirmed by the very word of God. The promise of God is that in the end God will make his home among humans and evil will be eliminated, but in our wildest dreams we cannot even imagine the positive dimensions of our new life with God. All the goodness our minds can conjure is finally not good enough to comprehend the glory of God's life among us. Unfortunately, to try to say more than this is to attempt to say more than Revelation is prepared to help us say. Fortunately, this is one matter in which God clearly has the final say.

The Gospel: *Matthew 25:31-46*

The Final Judgment of the Nations

Setting. The prophecy of the final judgment of the nations comes as the last section of Jesus' eschatological discourse in Matthew 24–25. The description of the end is a fitting conclusion for this part of the Gospel, for all that went before in the discourse pointed forward to this very scene. Immediately after this teaching, Matthew moves us into the story of Jesus' suffering, death, and resurrection. There is an appropriate irony in the use of this doomsday scene on New Year's Day, for as Christians look ahead to the new year, perhaps forming our New Year's resolutions, we should be mindful of the promise that God has the final say over our lives.

Structure. The story presents a clear and uninterrupted account that develops logically. "The Son of Man" appears in power. Then, he separates the individuals from all the nations, "the sheep from the goats." In turn, he addresses each group, first the sheep and then the goats. After each address by "the king," the members of the groups respond. When they have spoken in chorus, the king pronounces his verdict. For shaping a sermon in relation to the form of the text, it is crucial to notice the content of the sections as well as their order. The ideas inherent in the passage that should be treated in proclamation are (1) Christ is coming for judgment; (2) judgment means separation; (3) the standards for the division are striking; (4) both the sheep and the goats are surprised; and (5) Christ has the last word.

Significance. The news that Christ is coming to judge the nations should take no one in a Christian congregation by surprise. The New Testament states this conviction over and over, but what to make of the message? The most basic way to apply this text to our lives to take seriously that God is active, God has standards, so that not everything goes, and God promises to reckon reality and human existence in relation to God's standards. Since Jesus Christ is to act as judge, we know something about who he is, how he lived, and what we can expect him to do in God's behalf. As God's standards were revealed by Christ, they will be applied by Christ.

The idea of separation, goats from sheep, is difficult; but it is a striking part of the biblical vision and message. Again, not everything goes with God. Many of our actions and many of our attitudes have no place in God's kingdom, and through the judgment of Christ God effects a separation that purifies, that winnows, that establishes the right and eliminates the wrong. Remarkably, in Matthew's Gospel the notion of such separation is always held for the future. The present is a mixture of the kinds, but the promise of separation should startle us to examine our own ways before Christ does.

In this story we find a remarkable standard for the separation. Christ judges the peoples of all the nations in terms of whether they did or did not give food to the hungry, drink to the thirsty, hospitality to the stranger, clothing to the naked, care to the sick, and comfort to those in prison. We read nothing in Christ's list about a profession of faith, and indeed the last thing the sheep seem to have had was a personal relationship with Jesus Christ. This observation is not a slam at contemporary evangelical concerns, but it is a reminder that purely personal piety is not all that Christ calls for and expects. This scene of a final judgment is part of Matthew's total Gospel, and in that complete work there are other passages that balance this one with its heavy emphasis on social action. Moreover, Matthew's Gospel finds its place in the context of the canon of Scripture from which it is clear that a strong relationship between God and the human(s) is indeed a central part of God's purposes of working through the history of Israel and in the person of Jesus Christ. The heart of the gospel is that we have a relationship to God in Christ and, from that relationship, we find the directions for our living; both the relationship and the direction come by grace.

One of the curious elements of this story is that both the sheep and the goats are surprised. The sheep have served Christ without knowing him, and the goats have known Christ without serving him. The surprise in this final judgment is that Christ does not deal with those who both know and serve him. The lesson tells us about the fate of all but active Christians, so that we are given a pair of lessons: First, we learn of Christ's capacity to judge those who have never known him; and, second, we are shown that lip service is not enough. More than anything this text strives to startle complacent Christians into an active life of faith.

Finally, despite the surprise and the protests of both groups, Christ's judgment stands. Excuses do not work. Thus, clearly the authority for judgment rests with God, not with us.

New Year's Day: The Celebration

Perhaps the most popular service for New Year's Eve or Day is the Covenant Renewal Service, which comes out of the Wesleyan tradition but has now been adopted for use by other denominations as well. Two quite different forms of the service may be found in *The United Methodist Book of Worship* (Nashville: United Methodist Publishing House, 1992), pp. 288-94 and in *The New Handbook of the Christian Year* (Nashville: Abingdon, 1992), pp. 78-84. The idea of covenant should be particularly congenial to those in the Reformed tradition.

One of Charles Wesley's great hymns on the new year has never been very popular in the United States because of its unusual meter and rhyme scheme. With the popularity of rap, it may find a new birth. At any rate, developing their own rap rendering of the text for the New Year's service might be an intriguing challenge for the youth choir! Notice how the text picks up themes from all of the appointed lessons.

> Come, let us anew
> our journey pursue,
> roll round with the year,
> and never stand still till the Master appear.

> His adorable will
> let us gladly fulfill,
> and our talents improve,
> by the patience of hope and the labor of love.

> Our life is a dream,
> our time as a stream
> glides swiftly away,
> and the fugitive moment refuses to stay.

The arrow is flown,
the moment is gone;
the millennial year
rushes on to our view, and eternity's here.

O that each in the day
of his coming may say:
"I have fought my way through,
I have finished the work that you gave me to do!"

O that each from our Lord
may receive the glad word:
"Well and faithfully done;
enter into my joy, and sit down on my throne!"

A choral introit, to the tune Wareham, is the following lines from Philip Doddridge:

Great God, we sing that mighty hand
by which supported still we stand;
the op'ning year thy mercy shows,
and mercy crowns it till it close.

The same tune should then be used for the following response to the benediction at the end of the service:

With grateful hearts the past we own;
the future, all to us unknown,
we to thy guardian care commit,
and peaceful leave before thy feet.

Baptism of the Lord (First Sunday After Epiphany)

Old Testament Texts

Isaiah 43:1-7 is an oracle of salvation. Psalm 29 is a hymn of praise that celebrates the power of God over nature through the motifs of a storm.

The Lesson: *Isaiah 43:1-7*

Fear Not!

Setting. A central characteristic of Isaiah 43:1-7 is the exhortation to Israel, "Do not fear!" in vv. 1 and 5. Claus Westermann notes in his commentary on Isaiah that the phrase is not meant to be a psychological exhortation for an audience to muster courage, but that it is a divine action meant to banish fear. He goes on to note how there are two contexts in which fear can be banished. Both uses are probably employed by a priest in the context of worship. The first is theophany, where a priest would encourage worshipers not to fear at the appearance of God. See, for example, how Moses encourages Israel not to fear during the appearance of God on mountain Sinai in Exodus 20:18-21. A second context in which fear is banished is during times of lament when individuals (and later the entire community) are threatened by some kind of danger. Such a context may be framed as a situation of holy war. Isaiah 43:1-7 falls within this second category. Twice in this text fear is being banished, which gives rise to divine promises of salvation. Three questions provide the focus for interpretation. What is the situation that has given rise to fear? How will God banish fear? And, finally, why must God banish fear?

Structure. Isaiah 43:1-7 evinces an intricate structure. When the passage is viewed as a whole, it would appear to be structured into a series of repetitions. Note, for example, how the unit begins (v. 1) and ends (v. 7) by making reference to God as the creator of Israel, then how Israel is pictured as journeying both in vv. 2 and 6, and, finally, how the center of the passage explores the relationship between God and Israel in vv. 3-5. Yet within this framework, it is also possible to discern two distinct units that begin with the command that Israel fear not! When the focus shifts to this formula two oracles of salvation come into view in vv. 1-4 and 5-7, which contain many of the same elements even though they may not be in the same order: an assurance of salvation with the Fear not! formula (vv. 1*a* and 5*a*); a confirmation of salvation (vv. 1*a*, 3-4 and 5*a*); and a proclamation or divine promise about an imminent salvation (vv. 2 and 5*b*-6).

Significance. The best way to interpret Isaiah 43:1-7 in preparation for preaching is to return to the three questions that were listed above.

First, what is the situation that has given rise to fear? The larger context of 43:1-7 provides insight into the situation of the intended audience. Isaiah 42:18-25 is a trial speech against Israel, which underscores two points, one sociological and the other theological. The sociological point is the helplessness of Israel during the exilic period. They are plundered, are trapped in prisons, and are prey to other people, with no hope of rescue (42:22). This social situation provides the stage for a theological conclusion. As terrifying as Israel's social situation in the exile may be, their real enemy was God rather than the Babylonians. God was the one waging war against Israel, bringing about their downfall (42:25), which is the point of this text. God's warfare against Israel is the situation that has given rise to fear.

Second, how will God banish fear? Because God's holy war against Israel is the situation of their fear, it now becomes clear that a call to courage does not go to the heart of the problem that is being addressed in the Fear not! formula. Courage in the face of God's holy war is both stupid and futile. Only God can banish fear by reversing his holy war against Israel, and this is what Isaiah 43:1-7 is about. The text states that God will banish fear in two ways (through redemption and by being present with Israel) that provide the content of the separate Fear not! oracles. The first oracle is about the legal act of redemption. ("Do not fear, for I have redeemed you"). Redemptive purchases are rooted in Israel's family law.

These laws presuppose kinship relations and obligations in three areas: family members who have become indentured slaves can be bought back (see Leviticus 25:47-55), family property can be ransomed (see Leviticus 25:23-34), and even the bloodline of a family can be redeemed (see the levirate laws in Deuteronomy 25:5-10, where the next of kin has the legal obligation of carrying on the bloodline of a widow). One suspects that all three of these meanings are functioning in the two oracles: that God is ransoming Israel from slavery (the situation of the exile), buying back their land (the motif of the pilgrimage back to Palestine), and performing the levirate obligation (note the emphasis on offspring). The second oracle is about divine presence ("Do not fear, for I am with you"). This oracle follows logically from the first. God will dwell again with Israel when Israel is redeemed, and the very presence of God with Israel will chase away fear.

Finally, why must God banish fear, especially when we note that God initially created it? This third question is necessary for preaching Isaiah 43:1-7 because a simple juxtaposition of the trial speech in 42:18-25 and the salvation oracles in 43:1-7 gives the impression that God is whimsical. One moment God creates the fear by waging a holy war against Israel, while the next moment God banishes fear. These actions appear arbitrary, especially when we note that Israel is given no role in prompting the radical change in God's behavior, such as seeking forgiveness, or by performing some other cultic act of repentance. The divine banishment of fear merely happens in 43:1-17. The framing of Isaiah 43:1-7 with creation imagery provides a clue for the divine action in 43:1-7. Verses 1 and 7 underscore that God created Israel. Given the way in which this creation motif frames a series of divine acts of redemption, it would appear God's formation of Israel as a people implies a kinship relationship in which God has obligations. Thus holy war against Israel cannot be the final word, instead redemption must be. God has obligations that require the banishment of fear at some point, not because Israel necessarily prompts this action, but because kinship relationships are presupposed, which, in the end, outweigh all other considerations. In other words, God must banish fear. Verse 4 makes this very clear when God states: "You are precious in my sight, and honored, and I love you." Isaiah 43:1-7 would appear to be saying of God's character that blood is thicker than fear, that redemption has priority over holy war. Israel's responsibility in this context is simply to recognize God's act of redemption when it occurs.

The Response: *Psalm 29*

Celebrating the Power of God

Setting. Psalm 29 is a powerful hymn of praise. It celebrates the rule of God over nature through the motifs of a storm. The frequent repetition of "the voice of the Lord" (seven times in vv. 3-9) is best interpreted as thunder, which is accompanying a storm that has rolled off the Mediterranean Sea and is hitting the coast, from there it shakes the cedars of Lebanon in the north, before it swings southward to cast bolts of lightning in the southern wilderness of Kadesh. The imagery is vivid and ancient. Scholars have traced many of these motifs that celebrate the power of God in and over nature to the Canaanite culture that preceded Israel.

Structure. Psalm 29 follows the structure of a hymn, thus it separates into three parts: an introduction in vv. 1-2 that functions as a call to praise, an enumeration of the praiseworthy acts of God in vv. 3-9, and a conclusion in vv. 10-11, which both gives reasons why God should be praised while it also calls the worshiper once again to praise God. The hymn is tightly woven in its construction. For example, the introduction and conclusion balance each other with four lines, while each also refers to "the Lord" four times.

Significance. Psalm 29 is a celebration of divine power in this world, and as such it functions well as an extension of Isaiah 43:1-7, where the creative power of God was proclaimed to provide assurance to Israel in exile. Two themes in particular stand out as providing assurance to Israel. First, Israel and her neighbors had a tendency to divinize the power of weather because of its importance in their everyday lives. In this case, the psalmist uses a hymn formerly dedicated to Baal worship by taking on motifs from nature to celebrate the rule of God, specifically Yahweh. The psalmist has actually entered into a polemic about the character of power in this world. What appears most powerful to us in our everyday lives—

namely, Baal and the storms—may not necessarily be the case. Without such revelation the divine banishment of fear could never be seen by the people of God. Second, in view of the first conclusion, the psalmist encourages us to look for real power in this world in worship and not in our everyday lives. The introduction calls the community to worship (vv. 1-2) while the conclusion assures them of God's power in their midst (vv. 10-11). The introduction and conclusion provide the framework for interpreting the statement of faith about the power of God in the thunderstorm.

New Testament Texts

The readings for this Sunday are appropriately texts about baptism, given the focus on the Baptism of the Lord. Nevertheless, the Acts account is a peculiar story, wherein baptism and the reception of the Holy Spirit are seemingly out of sync with each other. In turn, the verses from Luke's Gospel offer a very placid telling of the story of Jesus' baptism. Both accounts come from the same author, Luke, and the awkwardness of the one and the tranquility of the other are intriguing; yet, when we examine these passages carefully, we learn something of Luke's subtlety as a narrator and something of the theology that he wishes to communicate to the reader of his Gospel and Acts.

The Epistle: *Acts 8:14-17*

No One but the Lord

Setting. Acts 8–11 is an account of the dynamic expansion of the Church in the wake of the persecution that came upon the Jerusalem congregation after Stephen came into deadly conflict with the Jewish authorities. Acts 8:4-40 focuses essentially on one of Stephen's fellow "Hellenists"—that is, Greek-speaking Jews—Philip. In Acts 8:4-24 we read of Philip's missionary work in Samaria. This account is laced with recollections about the magician Simon, the visit of Peter and John to Samaria, and the conflict of Simon and Peter. Verse 25 makes a transition; and then vv. 26-40 recall the encounter of Philip and the Ethiopian eunuch. As is apparent, our lesson is a snippet of the information about the earliest missionary work in Samaria.

Structure. The story we find in this reading is a straightforward narrative that progresses in a linear fashion. Verse 14 tells of the response of the Jerusalem Christians to Philip's successful preaching in Samaria; v. 15 recounts the actions of Peter and John in Samaria in praying for the Holy Spirit to come upon the new Samaritan believers; v. 16 explains the need of the Samaritan converts for the Spirit—they had "only" been baptized in the name of the Lord Jesus, not with the Holy Spirit; and v. 17 recounts how with the laying on of the apostle's hands the Spirit came upon the Samaritans in a dramatic fashion. In structuring a sermon in relation to this text one might think in terms of "taking note of the faith of others," "praying for the faith of others," "recognizing the necessity of growth in faith," and "acting for the benefit of the faith of others." In proclamation the preacher should never lose sight of the great distance between Jerusalem and Samaria—that is, the extreme animosity in the first century between Jews and Samaritans. In part, what we see here is faith coming to persons whom the Jerusalem Christians could hardly imagine as believers.

Significance. This portion of Acts tells a very peculiar story, which should challenge any interpreter—reader, teacher, or preacher. The story is difficult in a number of ways. The manner in which the events proceed, however, shows that there is no formula that may be invoked in order to ensure the reception of the Holy Spirit. This is particularly clear when one compares the following story of Peter's confrontation with Simon, who desires to purchase the Holy Spirit and to manipulate the Spirit's power for his own glory. We learn—in contrast to the sequence of events in other stories in Acts about belief, water-baptism, and the outpouring of the Spirit—that there is no orthodox set of actions that guarantees the gift of the Holy Spirit. There is no do-this-do-that and get the Spirit!

As the apostles arrive from Jerusalem and find the Samaritan converts convinced about the Lordship of Jesus and baptized with water, but without the anointing of the Spirit, a crucial truth is registered. The Holy Spirit moves through people at God's discretion, people do not move the Holy Spirit at their will. (Again, the following story underscores this point.) Luke tells us with this account that God moves dependably, but as God wills. Christian belief and practice are not strings attached to God that we can or may pull to derive desired benefits from our Creator. Moreover, there is no magic in baptism.

Coming as it does in the overall Lukan account, this strange story makes a profound statement about the authority of God in relation to humanity, especially persons of faith. At the outset of Acts the risen Jesus commanded the apostles to serve as his witnesses. Part of the commission he gave them was that they were to testify in Samaria. Yet it was not the apostles from Galilee who took the message of Jesus Christ to Samaria, but the Hellenist Philip. Through Philip's preaching the Samaritans believed, and through Philip's ministry they were baptized; but the Holy Spirit did not fall on these converts, rather the Spirit held back and forced the apostles to come into the work in Samaria, which they had avoided. The Spirit used the apostles to bless the Samaritans, and so factions of believers were united in faith despite their former differences.

In turn, this story about baptism and the Spirit reminds us that all Christians do not have to be exactly the same to be acceptable to one another. Whatever our ethnic origins, whatever the sequence of our spiritual growth, we are all granted whatever measure of faith we enjoy from the same Lord who unites us despite our very real differences. Thus, in reflecting upon this reading for preaching in relation to the baptism of the Lord, we should focus on the Lord who unites us in forgiveness.

The Gospel: *Luke 3:15-17, 21-22*

The Surprising Manner of the One Who Came

Setting. A portion of this lesson was encountered in the readings for the Third Sunday of Advent, so in part the comments below repeat some of the observations offered then. Moreover, a general introductory statement concerning Luke 3 appeared in conjunction with the Gospel lesson for the Second Sunday of Advent, so the reader may consult that material for more information on the setting of this lesson. More specifically, vv. 15-17 are part of a report of the content of the preaching of John the Baptist. Then, in the context of

John's ministry of baptism, we read of Jesus' experiences at the time of his baptism in vv. 21-22.

Structure. As is immediately clear, there are two distinct parts to the lesson: Verses 15-17 give John's "answer" to the christological curiosity of the people, offering a prophetic declaration concerning the coming Mightier One; vv. 21-22 recount the experience of Jesus immediately following his baptism when, in prayer, the Holy Spirit came upon him and the voice of God told him with clarity who he was. By combining these portions of Luke 3, the lectionary presents the preacher and the congregation with a "prophecy and fulfillment" scheme. Luke was a bit more subtle, however, because he separated these verses with the report of Herod's animosity toward and imprisonment of John the Baptist in vv. 18-19. It may be rewarding to ponder the distance between John's expectations and Jesus' experience, for from John's words we might expect the coming Mightier One to arrive on the scene breathing smoke and fire, but instead we find Jesus in prayer.

Significance. Verses 15-17 are part of the bold proclamation of John the Baptist reported in Luke's Gospel (3:7-17). In the lines before this reading, we are confronted directly with information about the Baptist. Then, the next verses of Luke's report of John's preaching removes the focus from the Baptist. We learn that when people wondered whether John could be the Christ, he took the initiative to inform those around him that he was not the Christ and that there was another one coming who was far greater than he. John's declarations reveal that his own divine commission was to function as a witness to the forthcoming actions of God which, as we learn from Luke's account, are focused in Jesus Christ.

John's preaching promises judgment, but we should never forget the surprising manner in which God's judgment was revealed—first, in a babe in a manger; then, through a bold ministry of compassion; and finally, through the revelation of the depth of God's love in Jesus' death on a cross. The dazzling power of God brought Jesus' resurrection, which was the clearest confirmation of the will and authority of God revealed in the person and work of Jesus Christ.

As we read or hear Luke's account, we should be struck by the relatively neutral manner in which he narrates these dramatic events.

103

The story invites not a sensational sermon but a reverent reflection. Luke simply tells us of the opened heavens and the descent of the dove and the declaration (clearly from God) from heaven. There is no amplification of these events; rather, one finds Luke merely telling of their occurrence. Thus, this majestic moment in Luke's account gently recounts Jesus' private divine confirmations of his identity as the Son of God. One sees that Jesus' post-baptismal prayer is the occasion of the vision of the opened heavens and the descending dove. It is, however, impossible to discern through Luke's retelling of the events whether the word from God was a public or a private declaration. This reframing of the events distinguishes Luke's Gospel in comparison with the other New Testament versions of this story.

This account of Jesus' baptism helps us understand the person and the work of Jesus Christ. The story tells us who Jesus is, the Son of God, and it gives us the evidence for this conclusion. More than anything else, this story informs us who it is that we shall follow through the course of the story that Luke will tell of Jesus' ministry, death, and resurrection.

Epiphany 1: The Celebration

The new calendar's emphasis on the First Sunday After the Epiphany as the Baptism of the Lord reflects the pattern of the Eastern church which sees the baptism of Christ, the beginning of his public ministry, as the first public epiphany or showing-forth of him to the world. The tradition of the Western church, which tends to restrict the use of the term *epiphany* to the visit of the Magi, is inclined to ignore the fact that there are many epiphanies recorded in the Gospels, so to speak of "the" Epiphany is something less than accurate.

The antiphons at morning and evening prayer for January 6 in the Roman Catholic Church make clear that the images are dynamic and should not be subjected to some static view of historical time. At morning prayer is sung: "Today the Bridegroom claims his bride, the Church, since Christ has washed her sins away in Jordan's waters; the Magi hasten with their gifts to the royal wedding; and the wedding guests rejoice, for Christ has changed water into wine." And at evening prayer: "Three mysteries mark this holy day: today the star leads the Magi to the infant Christ; today water is changed into wine for the wedding feast; today Christ wills to be baptized by John in the river Jordan to bring us salvation." Either could be adapted for use as a call to worship for today's service. Notice the repeated reference to the miracle at Cana. That will be next Sunday's Gospel reading, so the call to worship can serve to draw all three occasions together and help make the point that *epiphany* points to more than one event.

A threefold blessing may also be used at the conclusion of the service to bring the three epiphanies together a final time, as follows:

May Almighty God, who led the Wise Men by the shining of a star to find the Christ, the Light from Light, lead you also, in your pilgrimage, to find the Lord.

Amen.

May God the Son, who turned water into wine at the wedding feast at Cana, transform your lives and make glad your hearts.

Amen.

May God the Holy Spirit, who came upon the beloved Son at his baptism in the River Jordan, pour out plenteous gifts on you who have come to the waters of new birth.

Amen.

If last Sunday was observed as Epiphany, this blessing may be used all three Sundays.

Previous commentaries for Years A and B discuss recent hymns appropriate to this service, and the reader is referred to those. One hymn not mentioned is "Baptized in Water" by Michael A. Saward. It can be found at no. 294 in the Episcopal hymnal (1982), no. 492 in the Presbyterian hymnal (1990), and no. 362 in the Church of the Brethren and Mennonite hymnal (1992). Its opening lines, which connect "baptized in water" and "sealed by the Spirit," make it very appropriate in connection with today's New Testament readings.

The Old Testament lesson provides the basis for the hymn "How Firm a Foundation."

Second Sunday After Epiphany

Old Testament Texts

Isaiah 62:1-5 provides an eschatological vision of Zion—that is, Jerusalem—while Psalm 36:5-10 is a celebration of God's rule there and the security that it will bring to the people of God.

The Lesson: *Isaiah 62:1-5*

Calling God to Account for Promises

Setting. Isaiah 62:1-5 is part of a larger unit of literature that spans Isaiah 60–62. Scholars have interpreted Isaiah 60–62 as the core message of a later postexilic prophet (Third Isaiah), who has taken the message of an imminent act of salvation from Second Isaiah (e.g., from the late exilic period) and refashioned it into a distant future vision of salvation (e.g., the restoration of Zion at the end of time). Commentators have suggested that Isaiah 60–62 separates into three parts by chapters and that each of these three chapters divides into a lament and a word of salvation to counter the lament. The aspect of lament rises in these chapters because the historical situation to which the prophet is speaking does not correspond to the vision of salvation that is being described. These visions of salvation, therefore, are eschatological. In spite of the tension between the present and the future, it is important to note that the future visions of salvation dominate the laments concerning the present situation, even though our lectionary text for this week includes a prophetic complaint or lament. We might outline the three chapters of Isaiah 60–62 in the following manner under the heading, "A Proclamation of Salvation."

I. The Nations Will Worship at Zion (60)
II. The Anointing of a Prophet-Mediator (61)
III. The Renewal of Zion (62)

Structure. Isaiah 62 separates into two parts that combine to describe the renewal of Zion.

I. Zion Is Renamed (vv. 1-5)
II. Zion Is Restored (vv. 6-12)

The lectionary text includes the first half of Isaiah 62, which is either a complaint or an oracle of salvation, depending on who the speaker might be, a central issue for preaching this text. Who is the "I" in v. 1? There are two choices. One possibility is to identify the "I" as God, while the other possibility is to identify the "I" as the prophet. An overview of the text would suggest that the prophet is the speaker. Note the frequent third person reference to God or to the Lord in vv. 3 and 5 (as well as v. 6). If we interpret the "I" of v. 1 as the prophet, then the unit separates into three parts, which include both complaint and promise. Verses 1-2a are the prophet's charge against God and his decision to speak in place of a silent God. The prophet redirects his speech from God to Zion in vv. 2b-4a in order to proclaim her name change from "Forsaken" to "My Delight is in Her." The unit ends in vv. 4b-5 by providing the reason for the change of name in that God has once again turned his attention back to Israel.

Significance. Once it is determined that the prophet is the speaker, it becomes clear that even though Isaiah 62:1-5 is about salvation, it begins with a complaint. The prophet's complaint is that salvation should be much more evident in Jerusalem than it is. Frequently the absence of God's salvation is described with the metaphor of divine silence. Recall, for example, how the lament in Isaiah 63:7–64:12 (see First Sunday of Advent, Year B) ended with the prophetic question of whether God would remain silent. The assumption in Isaiah 62:1-5 is that God is all too silent and the prophet cannot bear it. Thus he complains to God and states in vv. 1-2a that for the sake of Zion he will not keep silent even though God may presently be

107

silent. The prophet then turns his attention to Jerusalem in vv. 2*b*-4*a* and audaciously speaks a word of salvation in place of God. The core of the prophet's message is that Jerusalem will experience a reversal and that it will be symbolized through a name change. The reason given for the name change in vv. 4*b*-5 is because of God's changed attitude toward Jerusalem, which will result in a marriage. The logic of the text is not really completed at v. 5, because we do not know why the prophet can act so audaciously by speaking for a silent God. Verses 6-12 provide this information (see Christmas Day, Proper 2, Year B). The reason why the prophet can be so bold as to speak for God is because he has a written copy of God's promises of salvation, which he not only believes in, but on which he is even willing to call God to task. It is for this reason that he places watchmen or sentinels (Hebrew, *mazkir*—literally, "those who bring to remembrance") on the wall of Jerusalem in vv. 6-7. Such persons appear to have been court officials in ancient Israel, whose function was to be the "recorder" (see II Sam. 8:16; I Kings 4:3; Isa. 36:3). The watchmen in this text, therefore, appear to be recorders who have the written account of God's promises to Israel, and their goal is to give God no rest until the salvation begun at Jerusalem is completely realized in all the details promised by God (v. 7). Verses 8-9 provide further reasons for the prophet's boldness. This section is presented as a quotation from God ("The Lord has sworn . . . "). The imagery suggests that the divine promise of salvation is being quoted back to God—perhaps by the recorders who have been summoned by the prophet. Verses 10-12 can be read as providing a conclusion to the chapter since these verses underscore the confidence of the prophet—that, indeed, God will deliver on the complete promise of salvation.

The Response: *Psalm 36:5-10*

A Meditation on Steadfast Love

Setting. Psalm 36 is difficult to classify. The problem is the shift in focus from a meditation on the wicked in vv. 1-4 to a reflection on divine righteousness in vv. 5-9. These two sections are brought to conclusion with a prayer in vv. 10-12. When viewed as a whole, the three sections do not appear to have a unified literary structure. Consequently some scholars classify the psalm as didactic in character, while others suggest that it is a literary creation written for devotional purposes. What ever way one classifies the psalm, the imagery of God's house in v. 8 suggests that the worship community is intended as the setting for its use.

Structure. Because of the sharp change in form, it is possible to separate Psalm 36 into two parts, which is in fact what the lectionary has done by eliminating the opening verses on the activities of the wicked in vv. 1-4. An outline of the entire psalm would argue against the separation of vv. 5-10, since it would appear that v. 10 is meant to begin the final section of the psalm. When our focus is narrowed to vv. 5-10, it is possible to read v. 10 as the conclusion to the preceding section. In this case the motif of divine steadfast love frames the psalm in vv. 5 and 10, while it also appears in the middle of the unit in v. 7.

Significance. Psalm 36:5-10 provides both a counterpoint and a sense of completion to the prophetic complaint about divine silence that begins Isaiah 62:1-5. When the Old Testament lesson and Psalm 36 are read together there is a movement from complaint to prophetic vision of Zion (Isaiah 62:1-5) to a meditation on the reliability of divine steadfast love (Psalm 36). The use of this psalm as a response to the Old Testament lesson actually takes the worshiping community beyond the future vision of Isaiah 62:1-5, for the imagery in v. 8 underscores how the meditation on divine steadfast love is taking place within the present time: "They feast on the abundance of your house."

New Testament Texts

The lectionary moves into ordinary time with these texts. The lesson from I Corinthians inaugurates a series of selected readings from the epistle that will continue up to the last Sunday after the Epiphany (Transfiguration Sunday). The Gospel lesson from John interrupts the sequential readings from Luke that occur through the Sundays after the Epiphany. Paul celebrates the complementary diversity of the spiritual gifts given to the congregation by the same

Spirit, the same Lord, and the same God. John recalls Jesus' first "sign" and tells the story in such a way that it symbolizes the all-surpassing greatness of Jesus.

The Epistle: *I Corinthians 12:1-11*

The Facts about Spiritual Gifts

Setting. Paul's letter to the Corinthians treats an amazing variety of concerns, all of which are related to the desire of the members of the church to boast of their spiritual superiority. Certain members of the church are quarreling and forming competitive cliques, each of which claims to be more spiritual than the next. As Paul portrays the situation, spiritual arrogance is tearing apart the body of Christ as one group and then another parades its spirituality. Paul's letter shows that he understands all this inappropriate behavior to be nothing more than destructive boasting.

From I Corinthians 7:1 we can see that Paul is in part replying to a letter that the Corinthians sent him when inquiring about their situation. The repeated phrase "now concerning" at 7:1, 25; 8:1; 12:1; and 16:1 probably introduces the topics about which the Corinthians wrote; so that our epistle reading is Paul's answer to the Corinthians' question(s) concerning "spiritual gifts." The remarks come in the larger section of 11:2–14:40 where Paul explains issues related to church order.

Structure. The paragraphing of the NRSV suggests there are two parts to this reading, vv. 1-3 and 4-11; but close examination of Paul's rhetoric shows there are three related sections in these verses. Paul introduces the topic of spiritual gifts and the Corinthians' need for basic clarification in this area in vv. 1-3. Then, in vv. 4-6 the apostle offers a spiraling threefold statement about the diversity of spiritual gifts on the one hand and oneness of God on the other. From this declaration Paul moves in vv. 7-11 to explain the diversity as being Spirit-given, for the good of the whole congregation, and Spirit-willed. Thus, the sermon may follow the lead of the text and take up the topics of the need for valid instruction about spiritual gifts; the reality of diverse gifts despite the oneness of God; and the source of, purpose of, and reason for the gifts.

Significance. In our world today, as in first-century Corinth, Christian people need an accurate understanding of spiritual gifts. The problem for some of the Corinthians was that they brought thought patterns and expectations from their past experiences in pagan religions into their life together as a church. Culture determined religious conviction and life rather than religious conviction determining life and the understanding of culture. While our world is not that of ancient Greece, today we have difficulty comprehending the reality of spiritual gifts because our culture reduces the nature of these gifts to the level of birthright talents or acquired skills. Paul insists, however, that the Spirit of God enables abilities that are neither the result of genetics nor the outcome of training. To illustrate, a woman who was regarded by all who knew her as a brilliant, eloquent, and clear Sunday school teacher often confessed that she genuinely feared speaking before groups of people and that given her actual preferences she would never say a word in public. Nevertheless, she understood that despite her natural disposition she had been given a spiritual gift, which she exercised freely. She knew that the Spirit, not she herself, gave the necessary insight, expressiveness, and courage that others acknowledged.

Paul continues by recognizing that different persons are given different spiritual gifts, but he insists—repeating his point in a slightly altered fashion three times—that the variety of gifts comes from the same God. In the context of I Corinthians Paul is battling a spiritual competitiveness among the Corinthians who sought to rank spiritual gifts and to criticize persons for having or not having particular abilities. By rooting all spiritual gifts in God Paul shows that theological unity harmonizes charismatic diversity. Since all gifts come from the same Spirit, Lord, and God, they are of the same origin and nature and are not to be viewed competitively.

Paul pushes this line of thought further in vv. 7-11, arguing that spiritual gifts are not only Spirit-given, they are given according to the will of the Spirit. Thus, Christians can be neither arrogant nor jealous regarding spiritual gifts, because the Spirit determined the distribution. Indeed, the Spirit acted for the good of the whole church in giving all the different gifts to the members of the community of faith. The one-same God works through the clear diversity of spiritual gifts for the harmony and unity of the whole congregation. The manifold spiritual gifts extend from the very unity of God and aim at achieving the unity of the life of the church as the gifts are exercised in a complementary fashion.

The Gospel: *John 2:1-11*

No Wine Before Its Time

Setting. John 2 contains two stories—one about Jesus at a wedding in Cana and the other about Jesus in the Temple in Jerusalem. The other three canonical Gospels tell of the Temple incident but not of the wedding. Thus we can see that these reports could have existed separately and independently. Yet John placed them back-to-back. Moreover, the Synoptic Gospels recall Jesus' cleansing of the Temple near the end of their accounts of Jesus' ministry, but John places the same story near the beginning of Jesus' work immediately after the story of the sign done at the wedding in Cana of Galilee. Careful study of John's overall story shows that the placement is deliberate. Indeed, the two stories in John 2 are set so that they interpret each other. Furthermore, John tells us that certain deeds of Jesus were "signs"—that is, manifestations of his glory that were meant to bring people to belief (see 2:11 and 20:30-31). Thus, from the beginning of John's account of Jesus' ministry, through the correlation of these two incidents, we know clearly who Jesus is and what his concerns are.

Structure. A quick attempt to categorize this story might identify this account as a miracle story. But we should notice that John never refers to Jesus' extraordinary deeds as "miracles" or "mighty acts" (the designation of such actions used by Matthew, Mark, and Luke); rather, John calls Jesus' accomplishments "signs." And this story goes well beyond the normal components of an ancient miracle story (problem, resolution, confirmation) in offering complex details and development.

Basically the story establishes a situation in which a difficulty arises (vv. 1-3*a*); then, John reports the odd conversation between Jesus and his mother (vv. 3*b*-4). A series of subsequent actions produces the solution to the problem (vv. 5-8), and through the introduction of the steward of the feast and the bridegroom we learn from the steward's comments of the amazing accomplishment of Jesus (vv. 9-10). Finally, John explains the nature and results of Jesus' deed (v. 11).

Significance. The key to understanding and, in turn, preaching this lesson comes in John's closing comments: What Jesus did was a "sign"; and through this manifestation of Jesus' glory his disciples believed in him. In other words, this story is concerned with more than the bald fact that Jesus turned water into wine. Moving us to believe or not believe that report is actually not the point of John's account. Rather, John writes of Jesus' glory and calls us to share the disciples' faith in him. When we approach the story from this point of view we have an angle from which to interpret the story and a goal toward which to develop a sermon.

At the outset of the story Jesus appears with his followers in a special, but everyday, situation. He goes to a wedding. Commentators regularly explain the significance of the extended marriage feast in ancient Israel. Not only was the time unique, the performance of certain duties of hospitality was a matter of the highest significance in terms of honor and shame, categories that defined reality in antiquity (much as success and failure do today). To run out of wine was more than a disappointment, it was a basic breakdown in relation to a social duty that established one as an honorable or a disgraced member of society. The host who ran out of wine was in danger of far more than being regarded as a party pooper or a tightwad; this kind of social failure was a complete loss of face from which one might never recover, and the stigma could extend to the family in subsequent generations.

In this context of crisis the mother of Jesus calls on him to alleviate the situation, but his reply is certainly strange. The statement in Greek is not so rude sounding as it appears to be in translation. Essentially, Jesus says (in paraphrase), "Is that our concern?" And in relation to the gospel of Christ one wonders, despite ancient perspectives, how concerned God really is about such trivial matters. Above all, this conversation serves to recognize that Jesus had an appointed time to which all his life was directed. And since ultimately he acts in astonishing power in this story, it seems that his "hour" has indeed arrived in some way.

113

Next, Jesus' mother (oddly, she is never named here) tells the servants to obey Jesus. Then, John tells the reader about the water jars. Jesus makes more wine than the people could ever consume. Several items here are important. In the context of this Gospel, the reference to the Jewish purification rituals is polemical. Jesus fills up and transforms the Jewish ritual, thus it is undone by being overdone. In first-century Christianity this polemic was crucial, but for us the realities of Jesus' excellence, newness, and generosity are the central points of the text. In our context today, this story is not a license to bash Jews. Rather, we may simply see that Jesus supplies for real needs in a manner that is better than even the best that went before, and he does so in abundance. To see this much is to "believe"; and as the Gospel tells us later, to believe in Jesus is ultimately to "have life in his name" (20:31).

Epiphany 2: The Celebration

A balanced appreciation for the importance of the image of wine is necessary for real insight into today's Gospel lesson. That is difficult to obtain in a culture that with the eyes of a Manichee sees total abstinence as a primary virtue on the one hand, or else from a more Bacchanalian perspective thinks winecoolers are a great thing. Informed preachers, before tackling John 2:1-11, are encouraged to read, mark, and inwardly digest Robert Farrar Capon's *The Supper of the Lamb: A Culinary Reflection,* particularly chapter eight, "Water in Excelsis." Also recommended for the commentary which accompanies the recipes is Jeff Smith's *The Frugal Gourmet Cooks with Wine.*

At the heart of the matter is the simple fact that both bread and wine become what they are because of the presence of life, yeast, which grows within them. They are for Christians signs of the new life that is to be found in Christ. That is why the Eastern church has always insisted on leavened bread for the Eucharist and why grape juice that has been boiled to death may not be a totally adequate representation of what Christian living is all about. One is reminded of the wag's description of the difference between Episcopal and Baptist communion services: the Episcopalians use real wine and the Baptists use real bread.

The celebrative and eschatological character of the Lord's Supper may also be emphasized today. John's Gospel begins with Jesus inaugurating his ministry at a wedding feast, and John's Revelation concludes with the marriage supper of the Lamb (Revelation 19:9). If the Eucharist is celebrated today, the call to worship could appropriately be:

> Let us rejoice and exult
>   and give God the glory,
> for the marriage of the Lamb has come,
>   and his bride has made herself ready.
> Blessed are those who are invited
>   to the marriage supper of the Lamb. (Rev. 19:7, 9)

A viewing of the motion picture, *Babette's Feast,* would be an interesting exercise for the preacher and members of the congregation who might be participating in a lectionary discussion group as a part of sermon preparation.

The contemporary hymn, "One Bread, One Body," links the eucharistic theme with that of the gifts of the Spirit, which is discussed in the epistle reading. It can be found in *The United Methodist Hymnal,* no. 620.

Third Sunday After Epiphany

Old Testament Texts

Nehemiah 8:1-3, 5-6, 8-10 is an account of the post-exilic leader, Ezra, reading the law to Israel. Psalm 19 is a celebration of the Israelite legal tradition, known as Torah.

The Lesson: *Nehemiah 8:1-3, 5-6, 8-10*

Celebrating the Torah

Setting. Nehemiah 8 is part of a larger unit of literature consisting of chapters 8–10 in which Ezra is the main character. These chapters present a variety of literary-critical problems. They do not appear to be original to their present context, since the memoirs of Nehemiah are the point of focus throughout chapters 1–7. In addition, the literary style of Nehemiah 8–10 fits better with the literary style and events that are narrated in Ezra 7–10. The reader is advised to consult other commentaries for detailed discussion of the editing process that may have resulted in the present organization of the text. When preaching Nehemiah 8 note that chapters 8–10 are organized to reflect some kind of covenant renewal ceremony by the post-exilic community. Nehemiah 8 recounts the reading of Torah and the celebration of the Feast of Booths. Nehemiah 9 sketches out a covenant renewal festival of confession in which Ezra reviews the history of Israel in an extended prayer, which concludes with a dedication ceremony. Finally, Nehemiah 10 summarizes the events and lists the obligations that Israel took on in covenant renewal. The lectionary reading for this week includes portions of the opening ceremony, which focuses on the reading of Torah.

Structure. The entire account of the initial reading of Torah includes Nehemiah 7:73*b*–8:12, of which the lectionary reading has isolated three portions: vv. 1-3 recount the spontaneous gathering of the people in the square before the Water Gate on the first day of the seventh month and how they request that Ezra read the law; vv. 5-6 describe some form of a liturgical process in which Ezra reads the law and the people respond; and, finally, vv. 8-10 give an account of how the Levites then taught the people about the meaning of the text. The shift in focus from Ezra reading alone in vv. 1-3 to the more inclusive "they" in vv. 8-10 has prompted some scholars to suspect that Nehemiah 8:1-12 may be the conflation of two distinct accounts—one, in which Ezra alone leads in the worship service, and another, in which the Levites as a group play a more central role. Whether or not the present text was originally two separate accounts—the combination of Ezra with all the Levites as leaders in the service, along with the central role of the people in prompting the reading of Torah in the first place—accentuates how this event must be read with a focus on the whole community, rather than on a particular leader.

Significance. Three motifs stand out in this text to provide a springboard for preaching on the significance of Torah in the life of the people of God: (1) the community focus of the event, (2) the importance on understanding what is heard, and (3) the need to act in light of having heard the text. First, several aspects of Nehemiah 8:1-12 underscore how the reading of Torah is a community celebration. As noted, the people are presented as spontaneously prompting the occasion in v. 7. Ezra does not summon them, they summon Ezra. Then, in v. 2, the writer is emphatically clear that all Israel was present for the reading, including men, women, and children. This inclusive focus is repeated in v. 3. In addition, the leadership of the service is blurred in vv. 8-10 from being simply Ezra to an inclusion of all the Levites. Second, the text is not simply concerned to present an account of the reading of Torah, but more important, it underscores the need for all present to understand its significance. Verse 2 introduces the motif of understanding as a reason for the inclusion of children in the occasion. Verse 8 returns to the topic by providing more detail on what it means to understand, and at least two things are mentioned: the clear reading of smaller portions of the Hebrew text (Hebrew, *meporas*, meaning "divide in parts" or "declare distinctly"; NRSV, "with interpretation"), followed by some form of interpretation so that the people understood what was read. Third, the goal of the occasion was not simply understanding but action. This is brought out in the closing verses with the contrast between weeping and joy. Once the people understand Torah they weep (presumably because they see how far removed they are from fulfilling it). Ezra's command for joy rather than weeping is one way to underscore how understanding alone is not enough. Joy in this case is not simply an attitude, but it takes on liturgical activity. The people are commanded to eat, drink, and to give food away. The text concludes with a statement by Ezra that the strength of the people is, in fact, in this liturgical activity of joy.

The Response: *Psalm 19:7-14*

In Praise of the Law

Setting. Psalm 19 is composed of two apparently distinct psalms. Verses 1-6 are a hymn that praises the power of God in creation. Verses 7-14 shift the focus from nature to the law as a source of revelation. The praise of law as a source of revelation is a fitting complement to the celebration of the Torah in Nehemiah 8:1-3, 5-6, 8-10.

Structure. Psalm 19 separates into three or four parts, depending on whether v. 14 stands alone or is included with vv. 11-13. The following outline will divide the psalm between the praise of God in creation, the praise of law in vv. 7-10, and a prayer of supplication in vv. 11-14.

    I. The Praise of God in Creation (vv. 1-6)
    II. The Praise of Law (vv. 7-10)
       A. The power of the law to transform persons
         (vv. 7-8)
       B. A summary
         1. The influence of law on persons (v. 9*a*)
         2. The value of law (vv. 9*b*-10)
    III. Prayer of Supplication (vv. 11-14)
       A. Request for revelation (vv. 11-13)
       B. Rededication (v. 14)

Significance. The imagery that is associated with the law in vv. 7-10 and the request of the psalmist for revelation in order to understand the law in vv. 11-13 make it clear that law must not be understood in legalistic terms. Torah is disciplined life itself. Note how the law is contrasted with different parts of the psalmist's body in vv. 7-8. The law that is perfect, sure, right, and pure can transform the psalmist by giving back life, bestowing wisdom, rejuvenating the heart, and enlightening the eyes. The result of the transforming power of the law on the psalmist is stated in v. 9*a*. It results in an enduring fear of God which is pure reverence. Such transformation provides a point of contact back to Nehemiah 8:1-12 where such power was celebrated. The praise of law in vv. 7-10 prompts the psalmist to request its power in vv. 11-13, and then to rededicate a life of faith to the pursuit of it in v. 14. This sense of rededication is given a liturgical setting in the covenant renewal ceremony that provides the larger framework for Nehemiah 8–10.

New Testament Texts

As the readings from I Corinthians and Luke continue, we encounter two important passages. The epistle reading offers some of Paul's most important thinking about the Church, and the lesson from Luke presents the first full example of Jesus' preaching to the people of Israel. Engaging ecclesiology and clarifying Christology are the subjects of these two texts.

The Epistle: *I Corinthians 12:12-31*a

"You Are the Body of Christ!"

Setting. Readers may consult the discussion of setting for the reading for the Second Sunday After the Epiphany for information concerning the situation Paul faced in Corinth. The epistle lesson for this week follows immediately after the verses for last week. Now, however, Paul elaborates his teaching about unity and diversity in the context of Christian community by introducing and developing his best-known eccesiological metaphor, "the body of Christ."

Structure. There are three broad sections in these verses. First,

119

vv. 12-13 introduce the image of "the body," referring to its many members who are, nevertheless, one body. Paul bases the unity of the Christian body on the oneness of the Spirit. Second, a highly illustrative argument concerning complementarity of body parts comes in vv. 14-16, mentioning the foot, the hand, the ear, and the eye along with the weaker, indispensable, less honorable and more respectable body parts. Third, in vv. 27-31*a* Paul turns from the body metaphor to speak directly about the God-appointed gifts of the members of the Church and their relative roles. This section ends with a driving series of rhetorical questions and a pointed directive. The outline of this reading is suggestive for preaching:

THEME: THE BODY OF CHRIST
I. Unity and Diversity in Christ
  A. Various gifts
  B. Unity of the spirit
II. Illustrations of Paul's Thought
  A. Various complementary functions
  B. Issues of honor and shame
  C. Mutuality in suffering and rejoicing
III. Unpacking the Argument
  A. God-appointed order
  B. Clear differences
  C. Proper ambition

Using a late nineteenth-century model of homiletics the preacher needs only to supply the verse of a hymn or a poem, and presto, a sermon!

Significance. The structure of Paul's thought takes one a long way toward developing a sermon, for much of what the apostle says in this reading is self-evident. But certain elements of Paul's remarks are obscure because of their metaphorical nature or because of the difference between his time and ours, and these items require further clarification for focus and force of proclamation.

The metaphor of the body of Christ has been with us for so long that it is familiar, but as a good commentary will report, Paul did not coin this image. Philosophers in Paul's day thought and taught of the cosmos as a body, composed of diverse but complementary ele-

120

ments. Paul gives this image a new twist, however, speaking of "the body of Christ." We should recall that it was the very body of Christ that was crucified in obedience and raised in demonstration of the power of God. To be the body of Christ is to live a life of obedience to the will of God, in recognition that as members of Christ's body we do not have or wield power, for that is God's alone. Our place in Christ's body is given us by God, and to live obediently—no matter our part in the body—is our ultimate call.

Moreover, v. 13 makes clear that the normal differences recognized by this world are not of final importance. Recognizable ethnic and social distinctions are subsumed to the Spirit in the Body of Christ, so that we live in a new relationship to one another, a relationship that results from the work of the Holy Spirit among us.

In turn, all Paul's talk about body parts leads into a reflection on the members of the body in terms of "honor and shame." In antiquity honor and shame were fundamental categories that qualified or disqualified persons and things from taking various places in society. When Paul talks elliptically of weaker, less honorable members (the portions of our bodies least likely to go unclothed!) he argues that God's values are not those of the world, God honors the shamed (God raised the crucified Jesus), and in the context of Christian community God most honors those members of Christ's body who are most dishonored and maltreated by the world because of their "dishonorable" Christian identity and action.

Thus, Paul lists the God-appointed order of the Church. This list is no hierarchy of power, privilege, and position; rather it lists the order of importance of service. Without apostles, those sent out with the gospel message by God, there would be no churches; without prophets, those who searched the scriptures and discerned the will of God, there would be no direction in the life of the Church; and so on the list goes. What Paul seems to do here is to list the gifts from the least to most flashy. The Corinthians (with their will to boast of spiritual superiority) were most likely desirous of the most flamboyant gifts possible, but Paul calls them to hard work and real service that edifies the whole Church, not merely gift-possessing individuals and groups. And so Paul concludes with a bold imperative, "Strive for the greater gifts!"

The Gospel: *Luke 4:14-21*

How Will We Welcome Jesus Christ?

Setting. We return to the sequential reading of Luke's account of Jesus' life and work with this lesson. In general Luke 4:14-44 tells of the beginnings of Jesus' ministry in Galilee. This unit of the Gospel is highly focused, for in 4:44 Luke already portrays Jesus at work in Judea. Within 4:14-43 there are two specific locations in which we learn of Jesus' activity: vv. 14-30 recall Jesus' being in Nazareth and vv. 31-43 focus on his work in Capernaum. Our lesson obviously comes in the Nazareth material and is, in fact, the first half of a story.

Structure. Luke builds a narrative bridge in vv. 14-15, which introduces Jesus' work in Nazareth, so that when we meet him there we understand that he is at work in the power of the Spirit and with the praise of the public. The story of Jesus' attending a synagogue service on the Sabbath begins with v. 16. Luke narrates the events in vv. 16-17 and, then, in vv. 18-19 there is a citation of Isaiah 61:1, 2; 58:6 in a modified form from the Septuagint. Verse 20 brings the lesson to a conclusion (but not the story!). The account of the incident continues through v. 30, so even for preaching the lesson suggested by the lectionary, one should read and study the conclusion of the account to be sure that the part of the story encountered here is understood in relation to the whole narrative.

The lesson falls naturally into four parts. First, Jesus appears. The story is entirely positive. He works in the power of the Spirit and with popular acclaim. Second, Jesus goes to Nazareth. Here, attending synagogue on the Sabbath (as was his custom!) he receives a further positive reception, for the hometown crowd gives him the honor of reading the scripture and commenting upon it for their edification. Third, Jesus reads a special section of Isaiah that clearly announces the inbreaking of the will and work of God in the moment of time in which he spoke. Fourth, we see the aftermath of the reading. Jesus sat to teach, and the assembly awaited his words with great expectation.

Significance. Two items form keys to the interpretation and proclamation of this passage. First, in comparison with Mark's story sequence, this incident seems oddly placed; and, second, by comparison with the original text of Isaiah, one finds that the citation here is very deliberately shaped to serve a clear theological purpose. Both items merit comment.

In Mark's account (which Luke probably used as the basis of his own enriched version of the story of Jesus' ministry) Jesus is at work in Galilee, especially Capernaum, for some time before he appears in Nazareth. Indeed, in the verses following this portion of the story (see v. 23) Luke's telling of the incidents in Nazareth seems to presuppose Jesus' activity in Capernaum, which in Luke's arrangement of the materials comes overtly in 4:31-43. What are we to make of this? Scholars suggest that this story in Luke (that is, vv. 16-30) functions as a frontispiece or as a programmatic narrative for the remainder of the Gospel. Thus, the preacher should understand that this text is both paradigmatic and a clue to all that will follow in the Gospel.

The phrases of Isaiah that are cited in this passage are quite noticeably rearranged in comparison with the original Old Testament text. This rearrangement provides a key to understanding the message that Jesus delivers and that Luke records. Jesus' own statement that the text is fulfilled in the hearing of the listeners is, however, the starting point for interpretation. In the person and preaching of Jesus we are to understand that God's declared purposes are fulfilled. With the appearance of Jesus, especially since he himself is anointed with the Holy Spirit, God has moved to free humanity. The freedom is freedom from sin, and it comes through the work of the Holy Spirit in and through the person and the work of Jesus Christ. Moreover, the mention of "the poor" and the variously oppressed in these verses is telling, for as we follow the account through Luke and Acts we see a gradual lessening of overt concern with the groups named here. Thus, we should understand that the proclamation is more concerned with Christology, soteriology, and salvation than with mere sociology. This is not to say that the text is indifferent toward social reality; rather, we should see that current social reality is not an ultimate category—it is being upset, undone, renovated, changed. Indeed, God's generosity in liberating forgiveness shows divine indifference toward, even rejection of, normal earthly values! This is no mere egalitarian ethic, for God's liberating action in Jesus motivates us upward toward Christ, not merely downward toward a lowest common denominator.

Epiphany 3: The Celebration

Although we begin today to read the Gospel and epistle lessons sequentially, the Old Testament lesson on these Sundays after Epiphany will be chosen because of some common theme with one of the other two, usually the Gospel reading. Last week the wedding imagery of Isaiah 62 was intended to relate to the setting of the Cana story in John 2. Today the public reading of scripture by Ezra in the book of Nehemiah anticipates Luke's story of Jesus reading scripture in the synagogue at Nazareth.

The report in Nehemiah 8:5 that when Ezra opened the book all the people stood up calls to mind the custom in some churches of standing for the reading of the Gospel. It is a practice that is now being observed in many Protestant congregations, in which case the pastor and people should understand clearly why they do this for Matthew, Mark, Luke, and John, but not for Obadiah or Philemon. It needs first to be understood that the practice of standing for the Gospel lesson is confined to the celebration of the Eucharist and not done in those services that are based on the daily offices, which may be said in private as well as publicly. To stand for the Gospel reading is not because those four books are somehow "better" scripture. It is not a literary critique. It is rather a symbolic activity that views the Gospels as an icon of Christ, a symbol of Christ in the midst of the assembly. So when the Book of the Gospels is being brought into the midst of the congregation, the people stand to greet Christ in whom all scripture is fulfilled. It provides a balance between Word and Sacrament within the eucharistic event: first Christ comes to the people in the Gospel, and then Christ comes in the eucharistic oblation (which, in parallel action in many churches, the people also stand for either during the eucharistic prayer or in going forward to receive). Standing for the Gospel, then, is part of the body language of the eucharistic celebration, and is not a part of the Church's practice for other services where the emphasis may be primarily instructional. In keeping with the content of today's Gospel reading, to stand to hear the reading is a christological statement.

A hymn exalting the place of scripture in the Church would be appropriate following the Old Testament reading if the psalm is not used. A paraphrase of Psalm 19:7-14, "God's Law Is Perfect and Gives Life," is no. 167 in *The Presbyterian Hymnal.* In relation to the Gospel reading, a recent hymn, "Word of God, Come Down on Earth" is particularly fitting. It can be found in *The Hymnal 1982* (Episcopal), no. 633; *The United Methodist Hymnal,* no. 182; and *Worship* (3rd ed., 1986), no. 513. Many familiar hymns pick up the themes from the epistle reading. Among them are "Blest Be the Tie That Binds," "Christ, from Whom All Blessings Flow," "Holy Ghost, Dispel Our Sadness," "Like the Murmur of the Dove's Song," "We Are One in the Spirit," and "Where Charity and Love Prevail."

Fourth Sunday After Epiphany

Old Testament Texts

Jeremiah 1:4-10 is the call of the prophet Jeremiah. Psalm 71:1-6 is a prayer of trust.

The Lesson: *Jeremiah 1:4-10*

A Prophetic Commission During Chaotic Times

Setting. Jeremiah 1:4-10 fits into the category of a call narrative (for a detailed discussion of this form see Year A, Proper 17). The term *call narrative* is used to describe how certain individuals are confronted by God to function in a specific task. Moses, for example, is called specifically to save Israel by leading them from Egypt (Exodus 3). Gideon, on the other hand, must rescue the Israelites from the Midianites (Judges 6). In his commentary on Jeremiah, R. P. Carroll has noted the very concrete tasks that tend to characterize call narratives, and, in view of this, he suggests that such texts might better be characterized as commissions rather than calls, since the word *call* tends to be a more abstract category about ordination. Commissions, on the other hand, concern a specific task by a specific person or group of persons for a specific time. A special priestly or prophetic office is neither implied in the commission, nor does ordination necessarily follow. Gideon provides a biblical example of this distinction, when he explicitly refuses to accept an office of leadership after his task is finished. Furthermore, because of the specific nature of the task in a call or a commission narrative, the confrontation between God and the designated person also tends to be very concrete. Moses is tending sheep when God addresses him from the burning bush, while Gideon is pounding out grain. These two examples illustrate how the commission itself tends to be rooted

126

in mundane experience so that it can be recounted by the one being called. The recounting of such specific experiences is often used by the person who is commissioned as a means of authenticating their call by God to the larger community of faith.

The distinction between a call and a commission provides important background for interpreting Jeremiah 1:4-10. This text falls clearly into the category of a commission, which leads us to expect that his call takes place at a specific time and includes a specific assignment. Yet the imagery of the text works against the expectations of the genre. For example, instead of a divine confrontation that could be anchored in Jeremiah's daily routine so that it might be recounted at a later date, the reader of Jeremiah's commission learns that God called him to his task in his mother's uterus. The imagery here goes against the very character of a commission. What can this possibly mean for interpreting the commission of Jeremiah?

Structure. Jeremiah 1:4-10 has many of the parts of the call narrative, but the order is not clear. One way to read these verses is to follow the expected sequence of a call narrative: commission (v. 5), objection (v. 6), reassurance (vv. 7-8), and sign (v. 9). But there are problems with this reading. The most central is that v. 5 lacks the verb "to send" (Hebrew, *slh*), which tends to be a formulaic element in commissions. It does occur, however, in v. 7, which suggests that perhaps this verse is meant to be the commission, resulting in the following structure: an introductory word (v. 5), objection (v. 6), commission (v. 7), reassurance (v. 8), and sign with a summary statement (vv. 9-10).

Significance. The career of Jeremiah took place within one of the most chaotic times in the history of ancient Israel. International political structures were collapsing around Judah, which, in turn, were challenging established social and religious beliefs. In short: it was a time when the mere repetition of orthodoxy was inadequate, and the call of Jeremiah in 1:4-10 has been constructed to alert us to this fact. It is a text, which, on the one hand, couldn't exist without tradition, since it presupposes the standard form of commission, even though it departs from the form in two ways: Jeremiah is never given a choice about participating in the divine commission, and his commission is not specific enough to fulfill the requirements to authenticate the prophet to the larger community. The aim of the following interpretation is to illustrate that these departures in form signal how the call of Jeremiah has been fashioned into a criticism of orthodoxy, and as such, it provides guidelines for living the life of faith at a time of crisis.

The prenatal setting of Jeremiah's call is central for interpreting this text. Although v. 5 clearly describes a confrontation (or perhaps better an introductory word) between God and Jeremiah, the prenatal imagery is for two reasons hardly the setting that one expects for such a confrontation: first, the setting is not a concrete occurrence drawn from the prophet's life, which could be recounted in order to validate his commission in the context of the larger community; and, second, the prenatal setting eliminates any real choice on the part of the prophet with regard to his commission, by removing the point of origin from his life experience. With regard to the second point, note, in particular, how twice the word *before* is used (Hebrew, *btrm*) to emphasize the passive state of Jeremiah with regard to divine activity ("before I formed you," and "before you came out"). The passivity of the prophet is further emphasized by the description of three divine actions toward Jeremiah in his birth process. God controlled Jeremiah's birth from conception (God knew [Hebrew, *yd'*] him in the womb), through labor (God sanctified [Hebrew, *qds*] him from the womb), and into his prophetic career (God made [Hebrew, *ntn*] him a prophet to the nations). The choice of these verbs with God as the subject (especially the Hebrew verb *yd'*, with its sexual connotations of conception, and, *qds*, which suggests a divine claim on Jeremiah already at his birth through its root meaning of being set apart) reinforces Jeremiah's lack of active participation in his commission.

The lack of active participation by the prophet creates tension with the expectations of orthodoxy, which are expressed by the prophet himself as an objection in v. 6. Jeremiah's objection is that he is too young and that he does not know (Hebrew, *yd'*) how to speak. These are his only words in the text and they are strongly silenced by God in v. 7a ("Do not say, I am only a boy"), and then divine speech takes over for the remainder of the text with a commission (v. 7b), reassurance (v. 8) and a sign (v. 9). The silencing of

128

the prophet reinforces the interpretation of v. 5, that the prophet has no real choice in accepting the divine call.

The interrelationship of three themes, in particular, will provide a point of departure for preaching. First and foremost, the call of Jeremiah provides an example of a divine commission that does not arise from any kind of prophetic experience. There is no concrete occasion that the prophet can recount to validate his task, which is required by the call form. This fact places Jeremiah in a critical relationship with his tradition, because the form of his call lacks the expected content. Second, in the absence of specific experience to validate his commission, the prophet turns to images of conception and birth to argue that the word of God has simply been implanted in him, and that because of this he has no choice but to speak it. Once again such vague criteria as a basis for authority puts the prophet in tension with the orthodox requirements of tradition to validate a commission with more specific experience. And, third, the vagueness of his commission is carried over into his task. What exactly does it mean to be a prophet to the nations, and how would either he or his hearers know when the task was accomplished? These three themes combine to underscore the ambiguity of Jeremiah's commission. He goes through the expected processes of a call, yet the prenatal context calls into question the very orthodoxy of the call process. The prophet's commission is neither anchored in a clear occasion, nor is he given any real choice about whether to accept or reject the call.

The end result of using a traditional call form to introduce Jeremiah, even while its meaning is blurred, is that the prophet is presented as an archetype of how the people of God live during ambiguous or chaotic times, when the simple repetition of orthodox answers itself becomes part of the problem rather than the solution. The call of Jeremiah is an important text for the contemporary church, which also finds itself in chaotic times. Two aspects of Jeremiah's call, in particular, invite further reflection for preaching. First, the call of Jeremiah illustrates how prophetic preaching and living at times of radical change can neither ignore nor simply be a repetition of tradition. Second, Jeremiah's call actually provides traditional guidelines for preaching during times of crisis. The passive role of the prophet and his inability to validate his call from concrete experience underscores, at the very least, how important it is simply to keep talking about God's salvation even when the source of authority, the concrete task of a commission, and its outcome might be unclear. In such a situation the mere act of speaking (of which worship is one form) may provide the link to a new formulation of tradition.

The Response: *Psalm 71:1-6*

A Prayer of Trust

Setting. Psalm 71 contains a variety of traditional elements, which make it difficult to classify. It begins with the language of asylum in v. 1*a* ("In you, O LORD, I take refuge"), which is used of persons taking refuge in the sanctuary. The psalm may thus be classified as a lament, in which the worshiper also demonstrates a strong trust that God is able to save.

Structure. The lectionary reading is limited to vv. 1-6, which could be divided into a section of petition (vv. 1-3) and praise (4-6). Each half begins with a petition that God rescue the psalmist. The difference between the two sections is that the second introduces language of trust and praise. These sections would most likely divide differently if the entire psalm were being considered and the reader is encouraged to consult the commentaries for an interpretation of the entire psalm.

Significance. The imagery of the psalmist having been taken by God from his mother's womb provides a strong point of contact with the call of Jeremiah. This similar imagery, along with the language of petition and especially trust, allows the psalm to become an extension of the call of Jeremiah for the worshiping community.

New Testament Texts

The epistle reading is Paul's beloved meditation on "love," perhaps best-known from being read at weddings; but as examination of the passage shows, it is neither mere passion nor matrimony that the apostle has in mind as he writes these lines. The Gospel lesson

brings to a conclusion the story of Jesus' inaugural sermon in
Nazareth, presenting a rapidly changing series of events that come to
a surprising conclusion, all of which confront us with the question,
"How would you receive this Jesus?"

The Epistle: *I Corinthians 13:1-13*

The Central Characteristic of Christianity

Setting. Readers may consult the material on setting for the Second Sunday After the Epiphany for information on the situation Paul
faced in Corinth. Essentially the Corinthians were parading their
spirituality—comparing themselves to one another and boasting of
their superior spiritual gifts ("mine's better than yours!"). Paul has
instructed them about orderly worship and appropriate relations in
the context of Christian community. He has called them to the unity
of mutual appreciation in the power of the Holy Spirit and away
from destructive competitiveness. Paul called the Corinthians to service. Now, on the heels of his exhortation in 12:31*a* ("Strive for
greater gifts"), Paul turns in I Corinthians 13 to show the Corinthians the "superlative way." In this context, Paul extols the eternal
value of love.

Structure. The poetic quality of this chapter causes interpreters to
refer to I Corinthians 13 as a "hymn on love," and one wonders what
resources inspired the apostle's reflection here. Whatever may lie
behind this portion of the epistle, the highly polished language and
rhetoric probably do mean that Paul drew on a previous composition—his own or that by another? Yet, he did not drop this chapter
into I Corinthians willy-nilly. In thought and development of argument, the material is vitally related to the issues Paul presents to the
Corinthians,

Paul's meditation on the superlative way of love moves in three
parts with an epilogue: vv. 1-3 identify the uselessness of striking
charismatic gifts that are practiced without love; vv. 4-7 declare the
essence and the operation of love; vv. 8-12 ponder the eternal character of love; and v. 13 states a conclusion, related closely to vv. 8-
12 but also epitomizing the entire meditation. As is often the case
the pattern of the reflection is suggestive for the structure and con-

tent of the proclamation: (1) the necessity of love as a motivation; (2) the way love is and works; (3) true lasting values; and (4) the superiority of love.

Significance. This is no abstract meditation on love, for in the context of I Corinthians one cannot help relating Paul's words to God, Christ, and Christian service. Love endures because love is the essence of God's own self as revealed in Jesus Christ, and love is now lived in the person of the apostle and by divine intention in the life of the Christian congregation. The talk here about love is exposition of what really matters in the life of a congregation. One minister reflecting on this passage said, "Paul speaks of his ultimate concern. A church with every vital program, but with no love, has a sheep dog not a shepherd. Paul declares the necessity of love."

One intending to preach in relation to this passage will do well to take pen in hand and make a few lists. For example, in vv. 1-3 what gifts does Paul mention? Conspicuous speaking in tongues, the discerning power of prophecy, complete faith, and selfless (sacrificial) generosity—all of which Paul says are useless without love. Paul is no spiritual pragmatist; the right kind of charismatic ends do not justify the wrong kinds of spiritual means. Gifts without love are capacities out of touch with God.

Then, in vv. 4-7, how is love defined? It is long-suffering and kind; it rejoices over truth; it is the foundation of reality; it keeps faith alive; it generates hope; and it is unquenchable! What does not characterize love? Envy, arrogance, pomposity, taking advantage of others, cautious self-service, boiling up in anger, holding a grudge, and viewing the sins of others with a smug sense of superiority. Illustrations abound for what love is and what love is not. Proclamation should not reduce love to being good; rather, the qualities named here are godly realities anchored in the very person of God. God's love extends into our lives, and in turn through us into our relationships with others.

With lists made, Paul goes on in vv. 8-12 to engage in a comparative exercise designed to establish through refined rhetoric the eternal quality of love. Any preacher will be challenged to match Paul's eloquence in her or his own translated meter. For reflection toward preaching we may ask, What is of true value in the Church today, especially from a Christian point of view? Sound teaching, an effervescent spirit, vital participation in the life of the congregation; a list of things and activities could go on. But we should see that the items on these lists come and go, whereas Paul says that the faith, hope, and love that provoke these things go on and on. Above all, Paul declares that the love that keeps faith alive and generates hope is itself the greatest of all—for as we can infer, love is the vitality of God.

The Gospel: *Luke 4:21-30*

Jesus' Startling Words

Setting. We considered the first half of this story last week, so readers may turn to the discussion of setting for the Third Sunday After the Epiphany for information on the setting of this reading. Before taking up this lesson in preaching, however, it will be crucial to remind the congregation of what went before in at least vv. 16-20; otherwise, v. 21 will provide an odd, potentially misleading, starting point.

Structure. The story unfolds as a series of panels. Verses 21-22 report Jesus' actions and initial words after he had read the scripture from Isaiah. Verses 23-24 record the favorable reaction of the synagogue crowd to Jesus' declaration and, then, recall Jesus' response to the response. In turn, vv. 25-27 are Jesus' sermon on the sense of the scripture and the meaning of his initial declaration in v. 21; here, he tells of incidents from the history of Israel to illustrate his interpretation of Isaiah. Finally, vv. 28-30 report both the hostile reaction of the members of the crowd to Jesus' preaching and Jesus' own activity in relation to them.

Traced thematically the story moves from (1) declaration of fulfillment to (2) positive reaction and recognition of its superficiality to (3) illustrations of the inclusive nature of God's care for humanity to (4) violent rejection of the messenger whose message called into question the hearers' assumptions about their privileged status to (5) recalling how Jesus was ultimately beyond the power of the crowd.

Significance. The crowd gladly heard Jesus' teaching that the promise of God's care for those who suffer and are oppressed was fulfilled. No one took offense at Jesus' implicit (bordering on being explicit) claim that the fulfillment was related specifically to him. In

133

the abstract the news sounded good, so Luke recalls that the crowd was impressed with Jesus, the hometown boy who had "made it," so they all spoke well of him. For preaching it may prove helpful to dwell on the way we in the Church today are like the synagogue crowd in Nazareth. We regard Jesus as one of our own. We hear many of his teachings as abstractions which, as such, sound good. And, like that crowd, we essentially assume the good news is for us.

Yet, Luke tells of Jesus' proverbial refutation of the assumptions—prophets are not really welcome at home; that is, true prophets may possess a vision that will jar our comfortable hometown assumptions. As an abstraction, Jesus' teaching was fine; but when he illustrated his point to make it concrete, the good news wasn't what was expected. God's favor and God's care are not restricted to a special group. We are not called to relate to God because of the benefits we will derive; we are called to God because of the magnitude of God's goodness. Rigid religiosity that lives with the expectation of privilege finds the news of God's universal love unattractive. After all, many ask, why bother to serve God if God is going to treat everyone the same? The call to the joy of a relationship with God seems too little, what we often want is something special. The news that God's love extends to all is offensive, especially to persons intent on being better than the rest and who expect God to recognize their goodness.

When Jesus' message proved to be different from what the crowd expected, indeed when his message turned out to run against the grain of their expectations, the crowd tried to rid themselves of this irritating disappointment permanently. Foreshadowed in the events of this story is the course of the ministry of Jesus. When he appeared on the scene he had a fine reception. Popular praise was the norm. But, with the passing of time, it became clear that Jesus not only did not fit popular expectations; in fact, he actively defied them. Then, people turned away, or they turned sour; and they actively turned against Jesus. The outcome of human hostility toward the message and the messenger of God's all encompassing love was seen in the form of a crucified man outside Jerusalem—a disappointment done away with.

And, yet, that was not the final word. In this story the crowd seeks to eliminate Jesus. But, mysteriously, he is beyond their power, and he goes his own way. Thus, we come to a foreshadowing of the Resurrection, which tells us that God has and will have the final word. Our power cannot thwart the love of God, expressed in Jesus, now raised in power and at work in our world.

In preaching this lesson, one must be careful not to create a gap between the past and the present. This story is not merely an account of something that happened long ago. Here we see the story of Jesus in its true timelessness. As they reacted, so we react; for we are a lot like the hometown crowd. But the good news is that the love of God is not defeated by our resistance. Instead, Christ lives and reigns and calls us ever anew to experience the abundance of God's love and care, along with all others.

Epiphany 4: The Celebration

Either of two traditional collects would be appropriate as the opening prayer which introduces the service of the Word for today. The first was composed for the 1549 *Book of Common Prayer* to accompany the reading of I Corinthians 13 when it appeared as the epistle reading for Quinquagesima Sunday (the Sunday before Ash Wednesday in the old form of the calendar).

O Lord, you have taught us that without love whatever we do is worth nothing: Send your Holy Spirit and pour into our hearts your greatest gift, which is love, the true bond of peace and all virtue, without which whoever lives is accounted dead before you. Grant this for the sake of your only Son Jesus Christ, who lives and reigns with you and the Holy Spirit, one God, now and for ever.

The other prayer was also included in the 1549 prayer book (Trinity XIV) from older sources:

Almighty and everlasting God, increase in us the gifts of faith, hope, and charity; and, that we may obtain what you promise, make us love what you command; through Jesus Christ our Lord.

The following common meter stanza by Charles Wesley will serve as a response to the epistle reading:

> The depth of all-redeeming love
> what angel-tongue can tell?
> O may I to the utmost prove
> the gift unspeakable!

The following passage from St. Therese of Lisieux's autobiography provides a guide for meditation on the epistle reading:

> This evening, after a barren period of meditation, I read this: "Here is the Master I give you. He will teach you all you need to do. I want to make you read of the science of love in the book of life." The science of love! The words echo sweetly through my soul. It is the only thing I want to know. Like the spouse in the Canticle of Canticles, "having given up all the substance of my house for love, I reckon it as nothing." I long for no other treasure but love, for it alone can make us pleasing to God. . . .
>
> That is all Jesus asks from us. He needs nothing from us except our love. God, who declares He has no need to tell us He is hungry, does not hesitate to beg a drop of water from the woman of Samaria. . . . He was thirsty!!! But when He said: "Give me to drink," the Creator of the universe was asking for the love of the poor thing He had created. He was thirsty for love! And now more than ever Jesus thirsts. From the worldly He meets with only ingratitude and indifference, and even among His disciples there are very few who surrender fully to the tenderness of His infinite love. (*The Autobiography of Saint Therese of Lisieux: The Story of a Soul,* John Beevers, trans. [New York: Doubleday, 1989], pp. 150-51)

This Sunday should occur near the beginning of February, Black History Month. Preachers will want to be particularly aware of relevant illustrations from the African American community for their preaching. The kind of rejection suffered by Jeremiah and Jesus can find parallels in the prophetic witness of African American leaders. Prayers should include thanksgiving for particular witnesses from that tradition.

Fifth Sunday After Epiphany

Old Testament Texts

Isaiah 6 is the call of the prophet Isaiah in the Jerusalem Temple. Psalm 138 is a song of thanksgiving.

The Lesson: *Isaiah 6:1-8, (9-13)*

Holiness and Atonement

Setting. Two aspects concerning the setting of Isaiah 6 are important for interpretation. First, it includes features of a prophetic call, and thus takes on the formal aspects of this genre, although the emphasis on a heavenly vision in Isaiah 6 is a new element to this genre (see also I Kings 22:19). Prophetic calls tend to follow a six-part sequence of action that consists of divine confrontation, introductory word, commission, objection, reassurance, and sign. (See the commentary on Exodus 3:1-15 for Year A, Proper 17 and from last Sunday for further discussion of call narratives.) Second, the setting of the call of Isaiah is clearly the Jerusalem Temple and the imagery picks up many aspects of the architecture and liturgy of the Temple. Note, for example, the enthronement language attributed to God in relationship to the altar in v. 1, the seraphs that surround the divine throne on the altar to form a heavenly council in v. 2, liturgical chanting in v. 3, and incense (smoke) in v. 4. The combination of prophetic call and the setting of the sanctuary provide the occasion to explore holiness and its two-sided effect on profane humans—death or atonement.

Structure. If the prophetic call of Isaiah is emphasized, then the boundaries of the text should be expanded to include the whole chapter. Even when this is done all aspects of the prophetic call do not appear in the passage (there is no sign). However enough features do appear to warrant an interpretation of Isaiah 6 as a prophetic call. Verses 1-7 constitute the divine confrontation and introductory word, which in the case of Isaiah is a vision in the Jerusalem Temple. The commission is in the form of a divine question in v. 8*a* that the prophet overhears. This is a departure from the expected form where God normally states a direct command to an individual (see, for example, Moses or Gideon), which then prompts objection by the one being called. Isaiah's call is playing with this expected form in two ways. First, as noted, he overhears a divine question rather than receiving a direct command. Second, having just survived a near death experience (seeing God and still living), he is overly motivated and volunteers to be sent out, when the expected form tells us that he should have objected. Isaiah then receives his commission, which is paradoxical. He must preach to confirm blindness in the people. In v. 11 the prophet realizes what he has gotten himself into and musters an objection, "How long O Lord?" The answer: until destruction is complete. The prophetic call of Isaiah is to confirm the guilt of Israel and thus seal their destruction, much like a manager who is hired for the sole purpose of shutting down a factory.

The lectionary text focuses on Isaiah rather than his call. And in particular the event of theophany, the danger of divine holiness for him, his realization of it, and his experience of atonement. Here the text separates into the vision (vv. 1-2) and liturgy (vv. 3-4), the prophet's recognition of danger (v. 5), and his atonement (vv. 7-8).

Significance. The root meaning of holiness is separation. When holiness is attributed to God in the Bible, at stake is the claim that God is separate from our everyday world. This notion has been carried through into more contemporary theology with the concept of God's "otherness." The distinction between the sacred and the profane arises from a recognition that God is holy and hence separate from our everyday profane lives. Sin is central to the concept of God's separateness. But sin in this case is more like the notion of pollution than specific human actions, even though human action might have prompted the pollution in the first place. The result of our actions is that we and our everyday world are polluted, and, furthermore, we have evolved in such a way that we actually need a polluted environment to maintain our lives. God, on the other hand, is not polluted and hence is fundamentally separate from us and our world. One can see here how holiness could prompt a very "otherworldly" religion. But that is not the case in ancient Israel. Instead, Israel confessed that the holy (and separate) God did not abandon this polluted world, but entered back into it by being enthroned in the Temple. Such mixing of a pure God and a polluted world is dangerous because the two are not compatible. Thus the holiness of God is dangerous to anyone and anything in the profane world, and the Temple with its liturgy is meant to provide a means by which the dangerous presence of God can be channeled safely into our world.

The dynamic tension and danger between the sacred and the profane is central for interpreting Isaiah 6:1-8. Notice how the distance (or separateness) between the holy God and the profane prophet is maintained in the opening verses. Although the prophet sees the enthroned God, it is only the hem of the divine robe that actually enters the Temple. Furthermore, the prophet hardly catches a glimpse of God before the focus changes to intermediary divine beings, the seraphim, who are themselves separate from God. These winged creatures, perhaps like cobra snakes with wings, cover their faces and their genitals, while they sing: "Holy, holy, holy is the LORD of hosts; / the whole earth is full of his glory." The content of the hymn goes to the heart of Israel's understanding of God. The first line underscores God's separateness, while the second line proclaims his presence. This is a dangerous situation, which the prophet immediately recognizes, "Woe is me: I am lost, for I am a man of unclean lips, and I live among a people of unclean lips." Note how sin in this case is pollution (uncleanness).

Fire is one of the central motifs in ancient Israel for conveying the danger that exists when the holy God enters our profane world. The motif enters the text in v. 6 through the image of a burning coal. The reason why fire is so often associated with the holy is because it is two-sided and hence dangerous: It can destroy or purify. This two-sided action is played out in the larger call of Isaiah. In the case of the prophet the fire of divine presence purifies him. His pollution is decontaminated, or to use the words of the text: "Your guilt has departed and your sin is blotted out." In the case of the people of

Israel it will lead to total destruction through a bonfire (vv. 9b-13, see especially, v. 13 "Even if a tenth part remain in it, it will be burned again . . . ").

Isaiah 6 provides a springboard for exploring the themes of divine separateness, sin as pollution, and salvation as atonement. The contemporary church has fashioned a casual approach to God. Central images today include mother, father, friend, companion on a journey. There is a strong biblical base for all of these images. But God is never a casual presence. The holiness or otherness of God needs to be proclaimed in the contemporary church, and our every increasing awareness of environmental pollution provides an excellent background for exploring the separateness of God from our world.

The Response: *Psalm 138*

A Thanksgiving Hymn

Setting. Psalm 138 is classified as a thanksgiving hymn proclaimed by an individual. Scholars debate who the individual might be, which then carries over into a debate about genre and Sitz-im-Leben (the cultic setting of the hymn). Is the individual the king, identifying this as a royal psalm, or is the singer any member of the community?

Structure. The psalm separates into three parts. Verses 1-3 are a song of thanksgiving in which the salvation of God is praised in the context of the gods (v. 1b). Verses 4-6 shift the focus from the divine realm to the earthly realm of kings. The psalmist underscores how all kings will one day praise God. The psalm ends in vv. 7-8 on a note of confidence. Because God rules in heaven (other gods) and on earth (kings), the psalmist expresses confidence in God's leading through this life.

Significance. Isaiah 6:1-8 invites a reading of the psalm in which the singer is any member of the community rather than the king, since it is the prophet who is confronted by the divine theophany. The psalm emphasizes the paradox that has been noted in Isaiah 6, namely that God is holy and transcendent (vv. 1-2), yet in spite of this he enters our world and even takes special note of our present life situation (v. 6).

New Testament Texts

Both readings present important traditions that have complex histories. The passage from I Corinthians 15 recalls the essential early Christian teaching about Jesus' death and resurrection, the very foundations of faith; and the story from Luke 5 reports an elaborate version of Jesus' calling of his first disciples. Thus, we come to important themes this week: the foundation of our faith and the call to discipleship.

The Epistle: *I Corinthians 15:1-11*

Recalling the Most Basic Matters

Setting. Repeatedly throughout I Corinthians Paul declares a topic and then proceeds to reflect upon it for the benefit of the Corinthians. For example, at I Corinthians 1:1 Paul refers to the report he received concerning the quarreling among the Corinthians and, then, he goes on to address this problem; and at 7:1 Paul mentions "the matters about which [the Corinthians] wrote" before reflecting upon appropriate sexual relations among the members of the church. In 15:1-11, however, Paul launches into the consideration of a problem that he does not name until 15:12—namely, that some of the members of the church in Corinth are denying there is a resurrection of the dead.

Apparently Paul considered the problem so severe that he "dropped back" in 15:1-11 to relay a foundation that he had previously laid in Corinth. Then, with this basic teaching having been re-presented, Paul will work off this foundation in relation to the problem in the remainder of chapter 15.

Structure. Paul introduces his presentation of the basic tradition concerning Christ's death and resurrection in vv. 1-2. Then, in the language of liturgical formulation, he presents the fundamental tradition in vv. 3-8. After delivering the tradition anew, in vv. 9-11 Paul applies the "meaning" of the teaching to himself and to the Corinthians. Thus, we find (1) introduction, (2) tradition, and (3) application/interpretation—a logical structure for a logical presentation. We should notice, moreover, that the traditional material in

141

vv. 3-8 is neatly structured: (a) death, (b) burial, (c) resurrection, and (d) appearances. Herein, the burial confirms the reality of the death as the appearances confirm the reality of the resurrection; and the crucial items, death and resurrection, are both said to have occurred in accordance with the scriptures.

Significance. This is a rich but difficult passage. Consultation of several good commentaries is crucial. The key to understanding what Paul is up to in these verses is to see that he is concerned with arguing for the reality of the resurrection. Thus, we should not be surprised that while Paul says Christ's death took place in relation to humanity's sinfulness and in accordance with the scriptures, he does not attempt to explain what he means. Christ's death and its significance are not Paul's concerns here, and while these issues are themselves critical, the present passage is perhaps not the one in relation to which the preacher should attempt to ponder the saving significance of Christ's dying.

Instead, let us follow Paul's lead and turn to Christ's resurrection. Paul declares with illustrated vigor the reality of the resurrection. The Christ who died and was buried was really raised from the dead. Paul knows this because the raised Jesus appeared to Cephas, to the twelve, to more than 500 disciples at once, to James, to all the apostles, and to Paul himself. Paul illustrates the reality of the resurrection out of the realm of wishful thinking, fantasy, or hallucination. The exact nature of the appearances is itself not Paul's concern, rather he argues for the reality of the resurrection through references to the several appearances of the raised Christ.

With the confessional line "in accordance with the scriptures" Paul reports the early Christian evaluation of Christ's death and resurrection. This understanding of the death and resurrection is the perspective of faith. Inherent in this understanding is the conviction that Christ's death and resurrection occurred according to the will of God. Paul's teaching about the reality of the resurrection declares that the power of God that raised Jesus from the dead mysteriously and mercifully made of his death a saving event that dealt with the sinful condition of humanity.

Moreover, the power that raised Jesus also transformed Paul, and Paul says it was at work transforming the Corinthians as they heard the preaching and believed. As the resurrection overturns the death of Jesus, it demonstrates the power of God, which transforms Christ's death into salvation as it transforms sinful human lives and saves through faith in Christ's death and resurrection. The reality of the resurrection shows the reality of the power of God, which alters reality itself—raising the dead Jesus, altering Paul the zealous persecutor into Paul the energetic apostle, and transforming the Corinthians from being people who were steeped in sin to be people who are being saved.

The Gospel: *Luke 5:1-11*

When Holiness Comes Commanding and Calling

Setting. The account of Jesus' ministry prior to his last days in Jerusalem runs from Luke 4:14 to 19:27. In relation to the texts from Luke 4 (the lessons of the past two weeks) we noticed that 4:14-43 recalls a period of work strictly in Galilee. Luke recognizes that Jesus moved beyond Galilee to labor among the Jews in other neighboring regions in 4:44, and at the outset of this geographically broader ministry we find that Jesus also moves from working alone to include disciples in his activities.

Our lesson is Luke's version of the call of the first disciples. It is instructive to compare this story with another telling of the call of the disciples in Mark 1:16-20. One sees immediately that Luke's narrative is more elaborate in content and structure. In turn, it is helpful to compare Luke's story with John 21:1-14, the account of a resurrection appearance which has striking similarities to this lesson. From these comparisons we should understand that Luke intends to communicate far more than that Jesus called some disciples or that Jesus once gave instructions that resulted in an astonishing catch of fish. Luke solicits an imaginative reading of this story, which should stimulate an imaginative (not the unbridled imagination, but the disciplined!) sermon.

Structure. In vv. 1-3 Luke establishes a situation in the life of Jesus which is not absolutely necessary for the story that follows, although it leads into it. The information here can be set aside for the purposes of preaching without loss. Then, vv. 4-7 refocus the

143

account by telling of an exchange between Jesus and Simon Peter that results in a seeming miracle. The recalling of the rich haul of fish is followed in vv. 9-11 by the report of Peter's (and the others') reaction, which invites a prophetic pronouncement by Jesus that results in the first disciples following Jesus. The themes that come forth in this story are Christ's commands, obedience, recognition of holiness and sinfulness, and the call to discipleship.

Significance. The general sense of this story becomes clear in Jesus' words to Simon Peter in v. 10: The story is concerned with the call to discipleship. In the background, however, lie several important matters that provide the backdrop against which Luke would have us understand the call itself.

Jesus came not only teaching but also commanding. Frequently his words (and deeds) seemed to fly in the face of reality. Such was the case when Jesus commandeered Simon Peter's boat, pressed him into service, and then, despite the previous night's work of fishless net-wetting, ordered him to cast off and try again—promising a catch! Who can miss the striking authority with which Jesus behaves? Such a Jesus demands and gets attention.

Luke reports that Simon was incredulous; yet, recognizing Jesus' authority, he obeyed. Notice the address, "Master"; and despite the protest, Simon recognized Jesus' power, "But at your word. . . . " The outcome of Simon's obedience was certainly more than the best he could have expected. The details of the catch in vv. 6-7 give special emphasis to its extraordinary nature. Simon and the others went from having nothing to having more than they could handle, all through obedience to Jesus' directions.

The reaction of Simon Peter to the catch is remarkable. He did not jump with joy, and he did not eagerly calculate his profit; rather, in recognition of Jesus' clear holiness ("Lord") Simon Peter realized his own sinfulness, and with honesty and humility he declared his own unworthiness—more exactly, he confessed his sin. The confrontation with holiness rendered the astonishing catch of fish irrelevant. With no mind for the fish, in the presence of the Lord Jesus, Simon Peter was painfully aware of his own condition. The provision of grace in the person and work of Jesus was simply overwhelming.

Jesus' words to Simon are also noteworthy. He did not ask him to

144

follow, and he did not issue a command. First, Jesus offered words of assurance to the sin-conscious Simon, "Don't be afraid." A rightful fear of the Lord does not produce paralysis. Then, Jesus simply spoke the truth of the future, "From now on you will be catching people." With the words of Jesus having directed Simon to the greatest success of his life, the recognition of the confrontation with Christ's holiness resulted in the transformation of Simon the fisherman into Simon the disciple and evangelist. And, there, on the verge of the greatest economic success of his life, Simon simply walked off from it all, recognizing the still greater worth of following Jesus. When Holiness came commanding and calling, through obedience and honesty Simon Peter's life was changed.

Epiphany 5: The Celebration

This is one of those few Sundays in ordinary time (Sundays after Epiphany and Pentecost) when all three lessons obviously share a given theme, in this case that of call as part of an experience of epiphany. Isaiah has a vision of God in the Temple, Paul is changed by his experience of the risen Christ, Peter sees himself in contrast to the holiness of Jesus. In each case as well, part of the epiphany is the sudden awareness of the disparity between the holiness of God and the sinfulness (pollution) of the creature. The good news in each case is God's ability to overcome the distance imposed by sin and to bring the sinner into a new relationship. That new relationship is epitomized during Epiphany by our Baptism, which imitates the Baptism of Jesus, and through which we are called to live out our faith during ordinary times.

The following stanza by James Montgomery could serve as an introit, a prayer for illumination, or a response to the Old Testament lesson. A short meter tune such as St. Thomas is recommended.

> O for the living flame
> from his own altar brought,
> to touch our lips, our minds inspire,
> and wing to heaven our thought!

The following prayer from the old Latin Mass was prayed before the reading of the Gospel. With slight alterations it could be used as today's opening prayer or as part of the act of confession. It could also be prayed solo by whoever reads the Gospel lesson immediately before that lesson with the people responding "Amen."

> Cleanse my heart and my lips, O almighty God, as you cleansed the lips of the prophet Isaiah with a burning coal, so that through your merciful cleansing I may worthily proclaim your holy Gospel. Through Christ our Lord.

It was standard practice in many Protestant circles a half century ago to talk about the order for public worship almost exclusively in terms of a paradigm that was based on Isaiah 6:1-8. The argument went that the service should first begin with adoration (vv. 1-4). Such adoration brings the worshipers to an awareness of their sinfulness before the God who is Wholly Other (v. 5), which results in a prayer of confession. Confession is followed by assurance of forgiveness (vv. 6-7), which enables the worshipers to hear God's proclamation and call (v. 8a) in the reading of scripture and the sermon, and to which they respond by a dedication of their lives (v. 8b). It is not unusual to see bulletins today that still divide the service into those components (Adoration, Confession, Proclamation, Dedication), whether or not the individual items under each category actually fit! Pastoral prayers and offerings, for example, rarely find their place as symbolic of the church's dedication in response to the proclamation. The paradigm is inadequate in that it does not make provision for the confession of sin to come as a response to the Word as well as being a preparation for hearing the Word. While Isaiah's experience serves one model, Peter's experience in today's Gospel lesson suggests another.

Notice the parallel between I Corinthians 11:23 and I Corinthians 15:3. In the first place, speaking of the Eucharist, Paul says that he "received what he handed on," and in the second instance, in a recitation of the kerygma, he says that he has "handed on what he has received." Both word and sacrament are part of the tradition into which he entered at his conversion. And his job has been to convey to others what he has received. This might be called living into and out of the liturgy. It is particularly noticeable in today's epistle reading, because the solemn, liturgical-like cadences, which sound like the recitation of a learned formula in vv. 3-7, suddenly give way to personal witness in vv. 8-11. Paul is affirming that by God's grace he has been made a part of all that went before. It is like repeating the Apostles' Creed and concluding by saying, "And I believe in the Holy Spirit, the holy catholic church, the forgiveness of sins, the resurrection of the body, and the life everlasting, because the Holy Spirit has made me a part of the holy catholic church by assuring me in baptism of the forgiveness of my sins when I died and was raised with Christ and entered then into the life everlasting." The point the preacher may wish to make about all this is that the liturgy is not a static "churchy" (ecclesial) thing, but it means, quite literally, the work of the people. What we say and do in church is but a practice run for the offering of our lives and work to God in the world. We are still being called with Peter to let down the nets, and with Peter we are overcome by what God can do with a little obedience on our part.

Sixth Sunday After Epiphany

Old Testament Texts

Both Jeremiah 17:5-10 and Psalm 1 reflect the style of wisdom sayings, in which the righteous and the wicked are contrasted.

The Lesson: *Jeremiah 17:5-10*

Two Ways of Seeing

Setting. Jeremiah 17:5-10 is best characterized as wisdom literature that has made its way into the present formation of the book of Jeremiah. One could read the unit as an independent poem or as a dialogue between Jeremiah and God.

Structure. The unit may very well consist of two separate poems. Verses 5-8 are a self-contained section that contrasts two types of persons. Verses 9-10 are a generalized statement about the unreliability of the human hearts. The catchword that links the two poems is the word *heart*. It occurs in the opening line of vv. 5-8 and of vv. 9-10. When Jeremiah 17:5-10 is read as a unit, it is best separated into three sections: the way that is cursed (vv. 5-6), the way that is blessed (vv. 7-8), and reflection on the human heart (vv. 9-10).

Significance. The central theme through Jeremiah 17:5-10 is trust. What do you trust in, how do you know what to trust in, and what in the end proves to be reliable?

Verses 5-6 and 7-8 set up a series of contrasts to develop the theme of trust. Each section begins with a direct statement about trust in vv. 5 and 7. The person who trusts in humans (Hebrew, *'adam*) is cursed as compared to the person who trusts in God and is blessed. The former lives by human strength (the power of flesh), while the latter lives by divine power. These initial contrasts end with a summary statement that the heart of the former has turned away from God. Then contrasting metaphors in vv. 6 and 8 draw out what it means to be cursed as compared to being blessed. To be cursed is to be a shrub in the desert, while to be blessed is to be a tree by water. The Hebrew word for "see" ($r'h$) is used to internalize the metaphor and thus personify the trees by illustrating how they contrast not only in their vitality, but also in their perceptions of the world. The shrub is so withered that it cannot see (Hebrew, *yira'eh*) the good, while the tree planted by water is so strong that it does not see (Hebrew, *yir'e*) or perhaps fear (Hebrew, *yira'*) the heat. By seeing the good and not fearing the heat the strong tree survives the drought.

Verses 9-10 begin with the voice of the prophet or a wisdom teacher who comments on the unreliability of the human heart. In its present context the statement is best read as an extension of the two different modes of perception, and, more specifically, it would appear to be commentary on the inability of the withered shrub to see good. When read in this way the comment is about the hopelessness of humans once they are cursed, because they are incapable of seeing the things that are reliable in life. The divine response affirms the hopelessness of such persons, while also noting how God will judge all actions. God tests the human mind; God searches the human heart; and, in the end, God judges human actions.

The Response: *Psalm 1*

Two Ways

Setting. Psalm 1 is a powerful example of didactic poetry in the psalter. Its language is reminiscent of Proverbs in general and Jeremiah 17:5-10 in particular. The clear indications of wisdom influence in this psalm, as well as its apparent absence in early numbering systems of the psalms (the Western text of Acts 13:33 quotes Psalm 2 as being Psalm 1), have prompted scholars to argue that Psalm 1 is meant to function as an introduction to the entire psalter. The psalm, therefore, may never have been intended to have a cultic setting for its use, but to provide a perspective in which to read the entire book of Psalms. The heading "two ways" arises from the sharp contrast in v. 6 between the "way of the righteous" and the "way of the wicked."

Structure. The contrast between the righteous and the wicked stated so sharply in v. 6 is central to the structure of the entire psalm. Verses 1-3 describe the way of the righteous, while vv. 4-5 (or 6 if it is not read as a concluding summary) provide contrast by describing the fate of the wicked.

Significance. Who are the righteous? They are first described in v. 2 by what they do not do. Notice the three verbs here, which follow a certain progression. The righteous (1) do not follow, (2) do not take the path, and (3) do not sit in the seat of wicked person, sinners, scoffers. Then what do they do? The righteous evince a constancy in life that is predictable because they have internalized Torah (v. 2). Thus, they are equipped for the long hall in life, and the writer underscores this point by introducing the motif of a tree with deep roots planted by a stream (v. 3). The wicked, by contrast, have no roots. Consequently, they blow with the wind (v. 4). The correspondence between this motif and Jeremiah 17:5-10 is striking.

The point of this psalm is not simply legalism. Torah in v. 2 is being understood in this context as Scripture, but even more, as God's moral structure for the world, which is able to provide meaning to human action for anyone who chooses to enter into it. Torah and Wisdom overlap at this point, because both are essential for structuring meaningful human action. The wicked person is one who rejects the structure of God's world. And here the point of Psalm 1 is the same as Jeremiah 17:5-10 when the two different perceptions of the withered shrub and the strong tree were contrasted. If a human being cannot see the good, that person will inevitably fear the heat and consequently not survive the year of drought. The human heart is unreliable when it is left on its own. Only God can provide reliable perception, which is done through divine testing and searching.

New Testament Texts

As we continue to move through I Corinthians and Luke we encounter texts concerned with the reality of the resurrection—of Christ and of Christians—and with something of the meaning of resurrection for life (I Corinthians) and with the disposition of God toward certain conditions of life in this world (Luke). The epistle

150

treats the theme of God's real involvement in all of human life, and Luke recalls, even reveals, God's judgment on particular elements of life.

The Epistle: *I Corinthians 15:12-20*

Christ's Resurrection as the Foundation of Faith

Setting. Readers may consult the discussion of setting for the Fifth Sunday After the Epiphany (last week) for an introduction to our reading for this week. The verses for this Sunday are Paul's frontal attack on the problem he faced in Corinth concerning the resurrection. Here the apostle builds on the foundation he laid in 15:1-11, and following the verses of this week's reading he will continue through the remainder of chapter 15 to discuss the meaning of his teaching in relation to the lives of the Corinthians.

Actually vv. 12-19 are a coherent unit of thought, and v. 20 is the opening line of the following section, vv. 20-28. But the reading suggested by the lectionary is sensible, for v. 20 states the "facts" over against the error identified in v. 12.

Structure. Paul's spiraling logic in vv. 12-20 is subtle. In v. 12 he states the problem—some Corinthians say there is no resurrection of the dead—and he indicates the basis of his own argument against their position—the preaching of Christ as raised from the dead. Verses 13-18 state a series of consequences of accepting the Corinthians' (erroneous) position: (1) Christ has not been raised (v. 13, repeated in v. 16); in turn, (2) the preaching of Paul and his companions is in vain (v. 14), and (3) the faith of the Corinthians is in vain (v. 14, repeated in v. 17); moreover, (4) Paul and his co-workers are guilty of misrepresenting God (v. 15); indeed, (5) the Corinthians are still in their sins (v. 17); and (6) those who died believing in the resurrection of Christ have perished (v. 18). In v. 19 Paul sums up the situation: If Christ is not raised and Christians are not raised, then Christian hope (Paul won't even use the word *faith* here!) is pretty pitiful stuff. Yet, v. 20 declares the truth of the gospel against the false position in Corinth: Christ has been raised as the first of all those to be raised from the dead.

Significance. In an indirect but forceful way Paul tells the

151

Corinthians that if they deny the reality of the resurrection of the dead, they deny the very foundation of the gospel—that is, the resurrection of Christ from the dead; and if they do this they should recognize that the Christianity they would embrace is not worth the bother. Paul can say this and say it strongly because he does not accept the validity of the Corinthians' position.

The power of God evinced in the resurrection of Christ and hoped for by Christians in relation to their own final destinies before God is the same power that transforms human life in the present world. If God does not overturn the ultimate work of sin which is death, then God does not forgive us and free us from the power of sin in this life. The Corinthians' denial of the reality of the resurrection was in essence a denial of God's concern with the reality of life itself. As they attended to the supposed superior spiritual dimensions of life to the exclusion of crass physical human existence, the Corinthians distorted the truth of the gospel—namely, that God is truly concerned with and truly involved with the course of our everyday lives. Indeed, the failure to associate the transforming power of God with every dimension of human life and destiny is a misunderstanding of God and God's purposes.

Paul's argument bites and stings as it turns the arrogance of the Corinthians' back on them in such a way that they are portrayed as being in the same position as those outside the Church, stuck in their sins. Paul recognizes that the Corinthians claim to be able to get along without God. But he knows no spirituality divorced from the reality of human life, and he tells the Corinthians bluntly that their perceptions are wrong, pitiful, and that indeed Christ is raised as the clearest evidence of the error of their thinking and the truth of the power and work of God.

The Gospel: *Luke 6:17-26*

Blessings and Woes in the Context of Christ

Setting. After recalling the initial call of disciples, with the clear recognition that such disciples would themselves engage in ministry (Luke 5:1-11, see last week's lesson), Luke continues to report Jesus' ministry of bold words and deeds. We see the power of God at work in and through Jesus, and we see the reservations and hostility that arose in response to him alongside acceptance and openness.

Our lesson this week comes immediately after one of the several special moments of prayer by Jesus in Luke's account (5:12). The result of this particular experience through prayer was that Jesus chose and named twelve special disciples, called apostles (meaning "ones sent out"). This action recognizes the time and nature of Jesus' ministry in relation to God's eschatological work for the salvation of humanity, for "the twelve" seem to symbolize "eschatological Israel," the very hope of God's promise of salvation.

Structure. The lesson falls into three sections—vv. 17-19, 20-23, and 24-26. The first section shows the charged atmosphere of Jesus' ministry. People came recognizing the striking character of his presence and work, and they came with great expectations—for the reality of divine power was clear for all to see. As the crowds came to Jesus, the second portion of the lesson recalls four "beatitudes" and a prophetic pronouncement made by Jesus. Then, coupled with these teachings, the final section records four "woes" stated in counterbalance or antithesis to the foregoing blessings. Thus, our lesson brings us blessings and woes in an eschatological context. For preaching one needs to "set up" the sense of expectation and urgency typical of eschatology and, then, in that context reflect upon the "points" of the blessings and woes.

Significance. The report concerning Jesus' ministry sets the stage for the following statements of blessings and woes. When Jesus came ministering, people clearly perceived the saving power of God at work in and through him. From near and far (anticipating the great universal character of the gospel) they came. With both physical and spiritual ailments they sought Jesus, wishing to touch him, to bring their lives into contact with him, that the divine power emanating from him might transform their lives. From these observations regarding vv. 17-19, one may ask how we perceive and approach Jesus today. Is the recognition of the vitality of God a "typical" perception of Jesus today, or has the perception of power grown faint? If so, why? Where in our world do people perceive the saving power of God in Jesus? How is it that some see and others don't? Where are we ourselves in the mix?

Verses 17-19 introduce Luke's version of the well-known "Beatitudes," which are coupled here with a set of "Woes." It is instructive to compare this portion of Luke with comparable materials in Matthew 5:3-12. There are four pronouncements common to the two Gospels, but Matthew's list contains five beatitudes without parallel in Luke. Scholars judge Luke's text to be more primitive than Matthew's balanced and elaborate passage. In turn, Matthew 23 contains an extensive set of "woes" pronounced upon "the scribes and Pharisees," but those woes are unlike the ones in our lesson.

Jesus' teaching here in Luke is not "dressed up" and it is very straightforward. Jesus talks of real poverty, of real hunger, of actual weeping, and of being hated and excluded. In relation to these terrible experiences Jesus speaks of the will and the work of God to overturn these situations. Poverty, hunger, sorrow, and oppression are contrary to God's purposes, and Jesus' promise is that these condemnable realities will not prevail. It is crucial to notice at least in relation to the fourth item—being hated and excluded—if not in relation to all these conditions, that the horrible experience comes because of the relation of persons to "the Son of Man." Fidelity to God may come at a heavy price, but God will have final say about the condition of those who are loyal!

On the heels of the blessings come the words of woe. As the blessings were pointedly related to reality, so are the woes. Jesus issues warnings to the rich, the full, those who laugh, and those of whom others speak well. From Jesus' own involvement with Zacchaeus, at banquet-tables, and in celebrations we should be wary, however, of concluding that he speaks here as the original mean-spirited Puritan. Again we must take these lines in relation to our disposition or fidelity to God. This understanding is warranted by the final reference to "the false prophets." Thus, Jesus says that if we live in this world forming our loyalties with an eye toward enjoying this world's benefits, we should be prepared to undergo God's judgments for our lack of faithfulness to God's own purposes.

The warnings here follow the promises of blessings, and we should see that in the first place the lesson issues a call to us to be faithful to a faithful God. Only in the second place, does the lesson warn us against false priorities. Thus, for preaching we should give emphasis to the positive dimensions of the text, although some recognition of the reality of God's eschatological judgment as well as God's eschatological salvation is necessary for a thorough engagement with this lesson.

Epiphany 6: The Celebration

A quick glance through today's lessons may lead to the conclusion that they basically offer two options for preaching. The preacher can either relate the Old Testament, Psalm, and Gospel for a sermon on trusting God rather than this world's goods and values or concentrate on the epistle lesson and discuss the centrality of the Resurrection for Christian faith. A third option, however, is to open up how the "good life" and its values—which turn worldly values and judgments upside down—are only possible for those who view life from the perspective of the Resurrection.

The danger of preaching some form of works righteousness is perilously close if we forget that Luke's list of blessings and curses is compiled on this side of the empty tomb. It is not only Jeremiah and Luke who speak today of the happy and the miserable. Paul speaks of how miserable are those who seek to practice the Christian life without belief in the Resurrection, and by implication (see vv. 57-58) how faith in the Risen Christ is the key to confident, victorious living. This is no "opiate of the masses," designed to persuade the hungry and the poor that they should enjoy it in hopes of something better later on. That is what happens when the Church preaches Luke 6 without taking the Resurrection into account. The Magnificat has already made clear that "Christ changes things," not always in a way that "those who make mere flesh their strength" (Jeremiah) are happy about. The Resurrection is an empowering event that enables us to embrace that ethic which is described in more detail later in Luke 6 and which will be considered next week. Put at its simplest, if we are going to walk around maintaining that God raised Jesus from the dead, then we are probably able to believe anything, even the possibility of loving our enemies and sharing more of our resources with the world's needy.

The emphasis on heart in Jeremiah (see commentary above) suggests the use of some form or part of Psalm 51 as today's prayer of confession. Notice not only "create in me a clean heart" in v. 10, but also the connection of heart and wisdom in v. 6.

The relation of Resurrection to social justice is made in Brian Wren's hymn, "Christ Is Alive!" See *The Baptist Hymnal* (1991), no. 173; Hymnal: *A Worship Book* (Church of the Brethren and Mennonite), no. 278; *The Hymnal 1982* (Episcopal), no. 182; *The Lutheran Book of Worship*, no. 363; *The Presbyterian Hymnal* (1990), no. 108; and *The United Methodist Hymnal*, no. 318.

Charles Wesley wrote the following stanza as a commentary on Luke 4:26, but it is equally appropriate for today's Gospel reading.

> The poor I to the rich prefer,
> If with thine eyes I see;
> To bear thy Spirit's character
> The poor are chose by Thee:
> The poor in every age and place
> Thou dost, O God, approve
> To mark with thy distinguish'd grace,
> T'inrich with faith and love.

(*The Unpublished Poetry of Charles Wesley: Hymns and Poems on Holy Scripture*, S T Kimbrough, Jr., and Oliver A. Becker-legge, eds. [Nashville: Kingswood Books, 1990], p. 90)

Seventh Sunday After Epiphany

Old Testament Texts

Genesis 45 is part of the Joseph story. In this narrative Joseph provides his brothers with a theological interpretation of the events that have befallen him. Psalm 37 is a wisdom poem that reflects on the different outcomes of wicked and righteous persons.

The Lesson: *Genesis 45:3-11, 15*

The Power of the Promise

Setting. Scholars have long since noted how different in character the Joseph stories are from the other ancestral stories. The sharpest point of contrast is the absence of God as a central character in the Joseph stories in contrast to the central role of God in the stories of Abraham, Isaac, and Jacob. God does not appear as a visitor at meal time, does not talk directly to people, and does not control the direction of events through supernatural intervention. Instead, the scope of the Joseph stories is more narrowly defined on the plain of human interaction within the family and in the larger arena of international relationships. The result of this more narrow focus is that God seems hidden in the Joseph stories, which raises the question of whether God is active at all. Where is the power of the promise to the ancestors in the Joseph stories? This question will provide the focus for interpretation.

Structure. Two different organizing principles are evident in Genesis 45. They are, first, the important role of dreams in the structure of the Joseph story and the placement of Genesis 45 within this structure, and, second, the outline of the passage itself.

First, the important role of Joseph's dreams and the placement of Genesis 45 in the larger structure of the Joseph story. Even though

157

God is for the most part hidden in the Joseph stories, the reader suspects divine involvement in the story through Joseph's constant dreaming. It seems as if dreaming is more natural than a waking reality, and it is his dreams that keep pushing the plot forward. The dreams of Joseph and their fulfillment allow the story to take shape in two parts. The larger structure concerns the initial dreams of Joseph in Genesis 37:5-11 concerning his family and the fulfillment of these dreams in Genesis 42–47. Within this larger structure, there is a smaller cycle of dreams and their fulfillment in Genesis 40–41. These dreams concern the Egyptian butler, the baker, and finally even Pharaoh. The two structures can be illustrated in the following manner.

(37)	(40–41)	(42–47)
Family Dreams	[Egyptian Dreams and Their Fulfillment]	Fulfillment of Family Dreams

These two structures are interrelated in the larger story because the dreams about Egyptians (and more importantly their fulfillment) in Genesis 40–41 set in motion a series of events which allow for the fulfillment of Joseph's initial dreams (in Genesis 37) concerning his family (in Genesis 42–47).

More can be said about the fulfillment of Joseph's dreams concerning his family in Genesis 42–47. This section of narrative progresses in two stages, with Genesis 45 providing a hinge: 42–44 [45] 46–47. Genesis 42–44 narrates two trips by Joseph's brothers to Egypt for grain. These stories have an undercurrent of trickery as Joseph toys with his brothers. Genesis 45 is a hinge because in this chapter Joseph discloses his real identity while also providing a theological interpretation of his brother's earlier treachery toward him. Genesis 46–47 completes the Joseph story by narrating how the family was reunited in Goshen. The analysis illustrates how Genesis 42–47 reverses the dynamic of disunity that characterized the opening story in Genesis 37 (see commentary for Year A, Proper 14 for discussion of Genesis 37).

Second, the structure of Genesis 45. The movement toward family unity that is evident in the larger structure of the Joseph story is also mirrored in Joseph's speech in Genesis 45. This reflection suggests that Joseph's speech in Genesis 45:1-15 is an important turning point in the larger story. His speech can be outlined in the following manner. The outline will include vv. 16-20 because these verses show the effects of Joseph's speech not only on his family, but also on the Egyptians.

I. Joseph Identifies Himself to His Brothers (vv. 1-3)
II. Joseph Provides a Theological Interpretation of His Journey into Slavery (vv. 4-8)
III. The Result of Joseph's Theological Interpretation (vv. 9-20)
   A. To the family (vv. 9-14)
     1. Father/son (vv. 9-13)
     2. Brothers (v. 14-15)
   B. To the Egyptians (vv. 16-20)

Significance. The hiddenness of God that has characterized the Joseph stories up to this point gives way in vv. 5-8, when Joseph identifies himself to his brothers in vv. 1-3, which then provides the context for a theological interpretation of his life story. Joseph states to his brothers that what they meant for evil, God has meant for good. This interpretation is not really very startling in terms of its theological content, the reader has suspected as much all along. Worth noting, however, is the timing of Joseph's theological insight. God enters the story precisely at the moment when Joseph also undergoes a transformation from being a powerful Egyptian, who is toying with a Canaanite family, to becoming their brother once again. The timing is not a coincidence, for it provides a strong message of how theological insight and proper human action often occur in tandem. The point is not to determine which of the two is prior— human action or theological insight—but to realize that revelation and ethical transformation are frequently complementary. Thus, whether Joseph's decision to make himself known to his brothers allowed him to see clearly the hand of God in his life story, or, whether it was just the reverse, namely that seeing God's hand in his life story gave Joseph the freedom to become a brother again,

doesn't really matter, because the end result is the same: The power
of God's promise breaks back into the story, which then pushes the
narrative in a new direction toward family unity in vv. 9-15.

Verses. 9-15 (16-20) pick up the motifs of family that were central to Genesis 37 (the opening chapter of the Joseph cycle of
stories). References to son (four times in vv. 9 and 10 [three times])
father (six times in vv. 8, 9, 13 [twice], 18, 19) and brother (five
times in vv. 12, 14, 15, 16, 17) dominate in the remainder of
Joseph's speech, and they are used to create a series of reversals
from Genesis 37. Instead of a story where there is no shalom (peace)
in the family, which then infiltrates the larger social and political
world (from the Ishmaelites and Midianites to the Egyptians), in vv.
9-20 these motifs create family unity (vv. 9-14, father-son; vv. 15-
16, brothers or kinship), which then affects the Egyptians in a positive way. Pharaoh is portrayed in vv. 16-20 as welcoming Joseph's
family to Egypt and as offering them the best of his country. By the
end of this story we no longer ask where the power of the promise
is, because we see that it has infiltrated every corner of Joseph's
world.

The Response: *Psalm 37:1-11, 39-40*

Trust in God

Setting. Psalm 37 is best characterized as a wisdom psalm because
it probes the limits of human insight and theological reflection. It
demonstrates the structure of an acrostic, which may have aided in
the memorization of the psalm, or served as a teaching device.

Structure. The most dominant device is the acrostic design, in
which every other verse is introduced with a letter of the Hebrew
alphabet. The internal organization of vv. 1-11 and 39-40 is difficult
to determine. The psalm presupposes that the audience (either a person or a group) is angry or at least upset about the success of wicked
persons. The speaker of the psalm is a wisdom teacher who encourages the audience to look below the surface before evaluating success or failure. Verses 1-9 address the audience directly with commands: do not fret (v. 1), trust in the Lord (v. 3), commit your way
(v. 5), be still before the Lord (v. 7), refrain from anger. Verses 10-

11 and 39-40 provide a summary conclusion to support the commands in the previous verses: The wicked will be punished (v. 11), and God will save the righteous (v. 39).

Significance. The wisdom teaching in Psalm 37 reinforces the message of the narrative in Genesis 45. The actions of Joseph in the Old Testament lesson embody the advice of the speaker in Psalm 37, which is that theological insight into the way that God has structured the world and proper human action must occur in tandem for humans to acquire wisdom. The advice of the psalmist is that the worshiping community organize its communal life around righteous actions that stem from God's character, and that in so doing the apparent sucess of the wicked will be seen as futile, precisely because it is not anchored in the divine character.

New Testament Texts

Two extremely rich and challenging texts form the readings for this Sunday, so that those approaching these passages for the purposes of preaching will feel initially overwhelmed by the materials that confront them. The reading from I Corinthians 15 is a treatment of the reality of the resurrection which pays particular attention to the necessity of the transformation that occurs through this act of God, and the lesson from Luke 6 recalls Jesus' teachings about the way in which people of Christian faith should live in relation to other human beings. The temptation will be to shrink back from the mysterious dimensions of the epistle reading or to reduce the Gospel lesson to a mere moral discourse. As a closer look at these texts reveals, these passages call the preacher to proclaim "deeper" things than slogans of "bafflement" and "be good."

The Epistle: *I Corinthians 15:35-38, 42-50*

The Reality of Resurrection

Setting. Over the course of the past two weeks we have examined the context in which Paul came in I Corinthians 15 to treat the topic of the resurrection. Readers may consult the previous discussions of setting for fuller information. In the verses for this Sunday we continue to follow Paul's spirited teaching. Now, however, the point of view shifts, as do the rhetoric and temperament of the lines. Earlier Paul presented the Corinthians' position regarding resurrection and argued that it was wrong. In v. 35, however, Paul introduces a rhetorical "opponent" whose imaginary questions attempt to undermine Paul's argument. Through most of the following verses of our reading (vv. 36-38, 42-49) Paul argues down the objection and carries on with further teaching.

Structure. There are three main segments to the reading with distinguishable subsections. Part one is v. 35, the imagined rhetorical questions in objection to Paul's previous teaching, and vv. 36-38, Paul's reply to the "opponent" which itself develops an argument out of agriculture. Verses 39-41 continue this line of thought but shift images, and they may be omitted as the lectionary suggests without loss of comprehension of Paul's position. With these verses passed over, however, part two begins with the comment in v. 42 which must now be understood to harken back to vv. 37-39 (though v. 42 really relates to vv. 37-41). From this start, part two continues as vv. 43-49 establish a set of contrasts (more on this below) that lead into an argument about the reality and necessity of a new resurrection body, different from that known during earthly life. Finally, v. 50, a brief third section, actually opens the final reflections in this chapter—that is, vv. 50-58. But, as part of the epistle reading for this week, this verse now summarizes or epitomizes Paul's argument in the previous two sections of our text. Paul's rhetoric and the content of his teaching are suggestive for the outline and lines of thought in an engaging sermon on the reality of resurrection.

Significance. Paul's imaginary opponent raises a sensible set of questions in relation to Paul's insistence that the resurrection is real and we know it to be real because Christian faith is founded on the proclamation that Christ is raised. "Will you tell us please a little more exactly what you mean and more precisely how resurrection transpires?" asks the inquisitor.

Paul replies through an analogy to seeds and the growth of plants to say that the earthly human body emerges in resurrection in a remarkably different form—but as a God-given reality. The analogy plays on the notions of earthly body, death, burial, resurrection, and resurrection body. Two items stand out in Paul's discussion. First, resurrection is not merely a metaphor for or a spiritualization of the idea of the rosy-glow aftereffects of a now-gone human life. Resurrection is not being remembered by family, friends, and community for all the good (or, bad!) one does in this life. Paul teaches that resurrection is a real, but dramatically different, existence in relation to God and others beyond the parameters of this world. Second, and more important, resurrection is a God-given reality. Humans do not persist past the point of death. No inner spark lives on now with the body gone. Nor do humans achieve resurrection. A dead kernel of grain is exactly that, dead. But, by the will and work of God, when planted the kernel comes into new life in the form of a new plant—as God grants such life. God gives resurrection life and body as God determines to do so.

In the next portion of the passage Paul sets up contrasts between the earthly and resurrection bodies which may be listed as follows:

Earthly Body	Resurrection Body
Perishable	Imperishable
Dishonor	Glory
Weakness	Power
Physical	Spiritual

These juxtapositions are not a lapse into Platonic dualism; rather, Paul points to the superiority of the anticipated resurrection body which comes as God's gift to those whom God raises. Here, Paul contrasts the reality of current earthly existence which is physical and affected by sin with the future resurrection body which will be spiritual, granted by God, and transformed by God's grace.

The ensuing typological argument regarding the first Adam (of Genesis) and the last Adam (Christ) is complex. Paul's basic point is this: As humans we currently share the physical nature and fate of the first Adam, we are sinners who die; but, by the grace of God in Jesus Christ, we are given the spiritual nature and fate of the crucified and raised Jesus, so that our present does not determine our future, rather God's grace does. Paul insists that the transformation from what we are to what we will be is necessary and takes place as God works graciously in and on our lives.

The Gospel: *Luke 6:27-38*

Living God's Love, Generosity, Mercy, and Forgiveness

Setting. Last week we encountered the initial verses of Luke's "Sermon on the Plain" (Luke 6:17-49), a collection of Jesus' teachings comparable to Matthew's more extensive "Sermon on the Mount" (Matthew 5–7). Indeed, the verses of this week's lesson may be compared with portions of Matthew's Gospel in the following way:

Luke	Matthew
vv. 27-30	5:39-42
v. 31	7:12
vv. 32-36	5:44-48
vv. 37-38	7:1-2

Examination of the materials in Luke in relation to Matthew, through the use of a Gospel parallel or by simply flipping back and forth between the texts, is instructive. Scholars conclude that both the Sermon on the Plain and the Sermon on the Mount comprise originally independent pieces of teaching that were later collected and incorporated by the evangelists into their respective Gospels. Both Luke and Matthew show some freedom in the arrangement of the materials, though Luke seems to have styled the form and vocabulary of the teachings to a lesser degree than did Matthew. Yet, Luke does seem to elaborate simple points for emphasis and clarity.

Structure. From the comparison of Luke and Matthew we see that the verses of our lesson fall into four parts. Any one or more of these subsections can serve as the basis for preaching. The boundaries established for the lesson by the lectionary, however, seem to suggest a repeated two-fold structure with the following themes:

- (A) Nonretaliation and generosity (vv. 27-30)
- (B) The Golden Rule (v. 31)
- (A') Further call to generosity, now based on divine character and the relations of Christians to God (vv. 32-36)
- (B') Elaboration of the logic of the Golden Rule with a

demand for congruity of life-style with expectations in
relation to God (vv. 37-38)

Observing this structure may be useful for preaching, but one should
see that the pattern—derived from the lesson suggested by the lectionary—is deceptive. In fact, in the context of the larger Sermon on
the Plain, vv. 27-36 treat the theme of love for enemies, whereas vv.
37-38 are part of the next coherent unit, vv. 37-42, which deals with
the theme of judgment.

In following the lead of the lectionary one faces the difficulty of
dealing with the different tones of vv. 27-36 and vv. 37-38—tones
which contrast because of the distinct concerns of the original units
of the Sermon on the Plain. The tension may provide stimulus for
creative reflection on the lesson from the lectionary, but for those
unable to resolve the difficulty (not an impossibility) a sermon on
vv. 27-36, or vv. 37-38, or even vv. 37-42 may make the task of
proclamation more manageable.

Significance. We cannot reduce these verses to morality, especially to
private morality. This is clear from the text. First, explicitly in vv. 35-36
and implicitly in vv. 37-38, we are called up to God's level in reflecting
upon this portion of Luke's Gospel. Second, the lesson always uses *you*
in plural form. Jesus talks of God, calls humans to God's ways, and
speaks to the disciples (see v. 17 and v. 20) as an assembly.

From these insights, the sense of the lesson is fairly straightforward.
The calls to nonretaliation, generosity, and mercy in vv. 27-36 are
based on God's own nature and on the assumed reality of the relationship of Christians to God. To be God's children is to relate to others as
God relates to us. Jesus' teaching here is essentially positive in thrust.

The tone and direction of the remarks change in vv. 37-38. The
call to nonretaliation, generosity, and mercy in the preceding section
was positive, an encouragement or an urging; although in the words
about only doing good to those who do good to us and about only
lending to those from whom we expect to receive, there was a gentle
warning away from *quid pro quo* living: It's ungodly. Now, however, in vv. 37-38 the tone of warning is amplified, so that a cursory
reading can lead to misunderstanding. Jesus is not saying "avoid
judgment in order to avoid judgment," "forgive to be forgiven,"

165

and "give to get." That would make absolutely no sense in relation to the previous verses, so that the arrangement of materials here leads away from misunderstanding. Jesus tells his disciples that what they expect of God, who Jesus tells them is generous and merciful, must determine how we relate to others. Again, Jesus' point is that if we are God's children, we shall live as God lives in relation to us. To know God's forgiveness and generosity means that we are ourselves God's forgiving and generous children.

Epiphany 7: The Celebration

The separation of verses within the same reading, as occurs today in the Old Testament and epistle readings, suggests how important it is that readers be familiar with the text in advance so that they may make the transition smoothly and not disrupt the flow of the narrative or logic. If books or leaflets with the lectionary text only are not available, readers should know the volume they are reading from sufficiently well to make the jump from one section to another. There is wisdom in typing the whole passage out in sequence so that it can be inserted in the regular lectern Bible and read from there. This also allows for larger print and for the passage to be rendered in breath or sense lines for the reader's convenience.

Although reference was just made to leaflets, their use by the appointed reader should be discouraged in favor of using a bound volume which by its very appearance suggests the reverence in which the Scriptures are held by the congregation. Such a volume may be brought in during the procession and taken to the place from which the lessons will be read. It should not have to compete with an ancient and unused pulpit Bible that sits ignored on a missal stand on the middle of the communion table, the ecclesiastical equivalent of the dust-covered but honored volume in the family parlor. If the Bible or lectionary is placed on the altar or communion table at the beginning of the service, it should be removed to the place of public reading and used at the appropriate time in the service. Otherwise all that is accomplished is a confusion of symbols concerning word and sacrament. We place a Bible we never read on a table we rarely or never use to celebrate communion.

Cowper's great hymn, "God Moves in a Mysterious Way," provides a poetic commentary on today's Old Testament lesson. Other hymns listed under the subject heading of "Providence of God" in most hymnals are also appropriate. Some, like "Sing Praise to God Who Reigns Above" and "We Gather Together" can do double duty by also serving as the opening hymn.

The epistle lesson's reflection on the reality of the Resurrection may be familiar to many congregants from years of attending funeral services where I Corinthians 15 has been a central part of the liturgy. Indeed, many may have heard it in no other context! This provides an opportunity to teach again about how the Paschal mystery is central to all we are and do as Christians, how each Christian funeral is an Easter celebration, and each Sunday a little Easter. It may also provide an opportunity to help people think about their own funerals as a last statement of Christian witness and to encourage them to begin planning their funeral services. Related hymns include "Easter People, Raise Your Voices" (could also serve as the opening hymn if the sermon relates to the epistle) and Natalie Sleeth's "Hymn of Promise" ("In the bulb there is a flower").

The very familiarity of many biblical texts cushions their impact for the hearers. That is certainly true of passages like today's Gospel reading. Imaginative and creative translations and paraphrases may be sought out for the proclamation, either in the reading or as part of the sermon itself. The Cottonpatch versions come immediately to mind as a way of changing the contours of hearing for the congregation. William Laughton Lorimer's work, *The New Testament in Scots* (Edinburgh: Southside, 1983), while not readily understandable to the average North American, will provide engaging insights into the text. In today's reading he translates "bless those who curse you" as "bliss them at bans ye." *Bliss* here is intended to convey the Scots pronunciation for *bless,* but the homiletical imagination should be intrigued by the coincidence that "bliss" can be defined as spiritual joy. The fun that one can have turning *bliss* into a verb is pure bonus! Notice also that *ban* may illustrate more clearly for modern hearers what it means to curse someone, to ban them from our society, our church, our nation, our fellowship. By that definition is it possible to hear the text as Jesus' advice about how those we ban are to treat us?

Last Sunday After Epiphany (Transfiguration Sunday)

Old Testament Texts

Exodus 34:29-35 is the account of Moses' shining face. Psalm 99 is a hymn celebrating the kingship of God.

The Lesson: *Exodus 34:29-35*

Ordination as Transfiguration

Setting. An overview of the larger structure of Exodus 19–40 is required when interpreting the Old Testament text. The first half of Exodus recounts Israel's slavery in Egypt and their rescue by Moses. These events follow a plot structure that is clear enough. Israel is in slavery (Exodus 1), Moses is born, raised in Pharaoh's house, kills an Egyptian and flees to Midian (Exodus 2–4). Then Moses returns with Aaron, goes through the long sequence of plague/signs (Exodus 5–10), before the events of the Exodus (Exodus 11–15), after which Israel begins their wilderness journey (Exodus 16–18). The story line stops in Exodus 19, when Israel encamps at Mount Sinai. Here there is no movement by Israel; no journey through the wilderness for roughly seventy-two chapters, until Numbers 10. Instead, all movement is vertical; it consists of Moses making trips up and down the mountain between God at the summit and Israel encamped below. This vertical movement by Moses on Mount Sinai is the key for interpreting Exodus 19–40. This section of the book of Exodus is probing the relationship between God and Israel by using the setting of a mountain. The Sinai narratives presuppose salvation (the story of the exodus in chapters 1–15), so that the central issue with Exodus 19–40 is how God will dwell with the people of Israel now that they have been saved. The mythological setting of the mountain, which is where the deity is located according to nearly any ancient

Near Eastern religion, alerts the reader to the cultic setting implied in these narratives.

Structure. Five times Moses ascends and descends the mountain in Exodus 19–40. The first time occurs in Exodus 19:1-8, where God and Moses work out the details of what will happen at Mount Sinai, which then provides an introduction for the remainder of the material. Distinct law codes are revealed to Moses in each of the next three trips (Decalogue in 19:9–20:20; Book of the Covenant in 20:21–24:8; Blueprints for the Tabernacle in 24:9–31:18), which would end the narrative if it weren't for the episode of the golden calf in Exodus 32. The whole story stops at this point because Israel has chosen the golden calf as their central cult symbol, which implies a rejection of God. Thus Moses breaks the tablets, which negates the process of revelation that has taken place up to this point. The story is in limbo in Exodus 33. The presence of God leaves the camp of Israel altogether (note how the Tent of Meeting is outside of the camp), and Moses goes into negotiations with God, which is an attempt to get the story moving again. Moses succeeds, and Exodus 34 narrates yet another trip by Moses to the summit of Mount Sinai, where he receives a new copy of the legislation that he had previously smashed. The Old Testament lesson provides the conclusion to the entire sequence of events by narrating Moses' final descent from Mount Sinai.

Significance. Exodus 34:29-35 is an excellent text for preaching on Transfiguration Sunday, for two reasons. First, Transfiguration Sunday is a celebration of God's descent into this world, which is exactly what the Old Testament lessons are about. Second, the primary way to communicate such a divine descent in the Bible is through the mythological symbol of the mountain. The vertical structure of the Sinai narratives has already illustrated this point for the Old Testament lesson, which provides important insight for reading the Gospel lessons where the same symbolism is employed to describe how God in Christ descended into this world and how the disciples (like Moses) were taken to the mountaintop in order to witness the revelation.

Several aspects of Exodus 34:29-35 are important for preaching. The first implication is the mediatory role of Moses. Moses has

169

assumed a special role throughout the book of Exodus. He alone was presented as encountering God on Mount Sinai in Exodus 3 through the burning bush, and this special role continues when all of Israel is brought back to Mount Sinai in Exodus 19. A central tension throughout the Sinai narratives is the fact that God is too dangerous to dwell with Israel at the base of the mountain. Thus the mediating role of Moses becomes a safeguard for Israel. The shining face of Moses is the result of his presence before God (see how God is characterized as a bright fire in Exodus 24:12-18). The writer is saying that, in a diluted form, Moses now embodies the presence of God for Israel. The reader or the congregation can tell at this point that Moses doesn't know his special function until he is told it by Aaron and the other leaders of Israel. The text confirms that one means of transfiguration in the midst of the people of God is through ordained persons.

A second strength in the text for preaching is the mask. There was a time when scholars interpreted the mask as a symbol of God that Moses would put on when communicating divine words. This interpretation is wrong. The mask works in just the opposite way. Moses' shining face so frightened the people (which is a proper response to divine presence) that he wore a mask to hide the light when he was not performing specific cultic functions of mediation. The text is very clear that Moses would take the mask off to receive revelation and (probably) keep it off to communicate the revelation, but then put it back on when the cycle was complete. The mask nearly replaces the function of the mountain in the earlier part of the narrative. Both symbols maintain distance between God and Israel by means of an intermediary.

A third implication drawn from Exodus 34:29-35 is that it is not a story about a distant and unrepeatable event in history, but a story about ongoing worship. The structure of the text illustrates this point. Verses 29-33 frame the event in the distant past. Moses, we are told, descended from the mountain unaware of his shining face, then after being told about it, he conveyed the content of the rewritten law codes before putting on a mask. Verses 34-35 build on this singular occurrence to describe an ongoing cultic practice. In other words the point of the story is to say that one way in which God is present and transfigured in worship is through specially ordained

170

persons, who, because of their status, are qualitatively different from the worshiping community. New Testament writers apply the content of this story to Jesus in order to construct a Christology, but these writers also single out a limited group of special persons, who, like Moses, also witness the events at the summit of the unnamed high mountain.

The Response: *Psalm 99*

The Enthronement of God

Setting. Psalm 99 is a celebration of God's enthronement in the Temple, which is the culmination of royal exaltation that occurs from Psalms 96–99. This praise can be likened to other enthronement Psalms 43 and 93, or royal songs in Psalms 2, 18, 20, 21, 45, 72, 101, 110, and 132. The king is addressed at his wedding or enthronement, but God is the object of praise, as the One who empowers the mediating king.

Structure. The psalm divides between vv. 1-5 and 6-9. Note how vv. 5 and 9 are nearly identical.

Significance. The two-part structure of the psalm provides further commentary on the issues raised in interpreting the Old Testament lesson. Verses 1-5 underscore how transfiguration is rooted in a confession of God's descent within the worshiping community, which in Psalm 99 is the Jerusalem Temple. The psalm goes beyond the Old Testament lesson by underscoring how the presence of God is characterized by justice and righteousness. This point was implied in Exodus 34:29-35 through the central role of the law as the content of what Moses received from God on the summit of Mount Sinai. Verses 6-9 emphasize once again how the descent and transfiguration of God in the setting of worship also implies a special status of ordination for those who will mediate between God and the people of God. In vv. 6-7 Moses, Aaron, and Samuel are highlighted as special priests of God.

New Testament Texts

The readings for this Sunday are selected with an eye toward the theme of transfiguration. The story of Jesus' transfiguration from

Luke's Gospel is an obvious choice, presenting the third of the Synoptic accounts of this dramatic event from the time of Jesus' ministry. The reading from II Corinthians is not so obvious. The coupling of this passage with the story of Jesus' transfiguration seems to depend on the references to Moses' "fading splendor" and the transformation of Christians by the power of God, which Paul declares with the words "being transformed into the same image from one degree of glory to another" (3:18). The central concern of the epistle reading is not with this "transformation," however, whereas Luke clearly intends to present Jesus' own transfiguration as an event of the utmost significance.

The Epistle: *II Corinthians 3:12–4:2*

Free in Christ unto Boldness for God

Setting. The situation behind the writing of II Corinthians is very different from that which led to the composition of I Corinthians. Sometime after Paul wrote I Corinthians, a group of outsiders arrived in Corinth. These people were Christian preachers, but their message was that Christianity was a vitally renewed Judaism wherein certain people possess the power to work miracles. These preachers claimed to possess that extraordinary power, indeed they maintained they were sources of divine power. Paul referred to these people as "super-apostles," a clearly sarcastic designation in the apostle's use, but a title that may have been their self-designation. Although the super-apostles clearly came from Jewish-Christian circles, they were like other Hellenistic religious propagandists of that day who had a flashy, obviously powerful style of ministry—powerful in proclamation and powerful in deeds.

There are distinguishable sections to II Corinthians. The recognizable portions of the letter are so distinct that many scholars conclude that the canonical letter is a later editor's compilation of preserved passages (fragments?) from more than one earlier letter. Whether or not that is the case, the section of II Corinthians from 2:14–6:13 (or 7:4) is an impassioned plea with the Corinthians in which Paul explains that the character of his ministry is consistent with the character of the gospel. Within II Corinthians 2:14–7:4 we find a section of introduction (2:14–3:6), a discussion proper of the substance and style of Paul's ministry (3:7–5:21), and a section of hortatory materials (6:1–7:4). The verses of our reading come near the beginning of the overt discussion of Paul's ministry. In reading this passage it is important to recall that Paul is responding to a cross fire of criticism from both the so-called super-apostles and some members of the Corinthian congregation.

Structure. In Paul's discussion of his ministry, II Corinthians 3:7–4:6 is a four-part reflection on ministry in the contexts of "the old covenant" and "in Christ." Our reading comprises parts two (3:12-13), three (3:14-18), and the beginning of part four (4:1-2). The opening of the lesson certainly builds off the foregoing remarks in 3:7-11 as is evident from the words "Since, then" at the beginning of 3:12; and what follows our reading in 4:3-14 is further clarification of the thought of our text as we see from the opening of 4:3, "And even if. . . ."

Paul's logic is difficult to follow, in part because of the strange statements about Moses and the veil. In effect, he argues in a loop. He begins with a statement about the boldness of genuine apostles, moves to the inferior situation of those involved in "the old covenant," declares the freedom established in Christ the Lord, and then restates the boldness (or, enthusiasm and openness) that characterizes the work of true apostles. At the beginning of this reflection Paul mentions the "hope" (of the ministry of justification), which generates "great boldness," and at the end of the reading he speaks of "God's mercy," which produces ministry in which the apostles "do not lose heart."

Significance. It is crucial to recognize that Paul is debating against other Jewish-Christian missionaries, not against Jews directly. The polemical tone of the remarks about Moses, the veil, and the blindness of those reading the old covenant are all parts of Paul's argument against the so-called super-apostles who had criticized Paul and turned some of the Corinthians against him and his colleagues. Thus, when we think about this text and the way in which it is relevant to our work in Christian ministry today, we must think in relation to those who criticize a forthright style of ministry because it lacks a conspicuous kind of pizzazz or spectacle.

It is quick and perhaps too easy to draw analogies to the ever present flamboyant televangelists who seem never to tire either of declaring their superiority or of criticizing those whose convictions and actions are not exactly the same as theirs. Readers need little help here. But can it be that Paul's reflection in our epistle reading hits somewhere closer to home than the television set? Basically Paul's retort to the super-apostles is a reply to any and all who blithely parade the superiority of their own efforts over against the work of others. Paul's remarks are relevant to all forms of religious self-satisfaction and self-righteousness, be it that of conservative, moderate, or liberal Christians. At root the problem Paul addresses is contentment that is based purely in the self—that is, in one's or one's own group's accomplishments. Paul says such an attitude is blindness, and he calls the Corinthians to a full-fledged recognition of the freedom granted by and in Christ, which moves us away from preoccupation with ourselves to devotion, trust, and active commitment to our God. With a variety of theological and social sensibilities in the context of Christian community, perhaps we should recognize that freedom in Christ may mean, above all else, freedom from preoccupation with ourselves and merely our own ways.

The Gospel: *Luke 9:28-36*

A Glimpse of Forthcoming Glory

Setting. Luke joins Matthew and Mark in telling of Jesus' transfiguration. He locates the events at a similar point in the course of his account of Jesus' ministry, although the volume of special material presented in Luke 9:51–19:27 gives the false impression that Luke came to this story earlier in his overall narrative than did Mark and even Matthew. Certain details of Luke's version of this account distinguish his story from those of Matthew and Mark, and while the preponderance of the narrative seems the same, Luke's particular direction in storytelling makes his primary purpose(s) perceptible.

Structure. The story is a gently told narrative that recalls a remarkable, symbol-laden series of events: Jesus takes three special disciples up the mountain to pray; he prays and is transfigured;

Moses and Elijah appear in glory and speak with Jesus about his "departure" in Jerusalem; Peter and the other two disciples were nearly overcome with sleep but they stayed awake and saw "the glory"; Peter speaks, somewhat ignorantly; a cloud comes and engulfs Jesus, Moses, and Elijah; a voice speaks; Jesus remains alone with the disciples; and they remained silent concerning what they saw. The Transfiguration per se is the center of the account, but we find many indications of the message Luke intends for this narrative as we ponder the many incidents and details reported.

Significance. This is a story about the revelation of Jesus' divine glory, which was seen by some in the course of his earthly ministry, but which found fulfillment and full meaning only in relation to his death, resurrection, and ascension. All persons planning to preach on this vital text (and not all great preachers have chosen to do so) should carefully read and compare the three Gospel accounts (a fourth allusion to the incident appears in II Peter 1:16-18). Each author has a perspective on the events on the mountain, and preachers will do well to take seriously the evangelists' points of view and to avoid a harmonized retelling that faithfully reflects none of the New Testament accounts.

Luke opens the story with a temporal notice, "Now about eight days after these sayings. . . ." Matthew and Mark mention "six" days. Why the difference? In early Christianity the "eighth day" was a way of speaking of the "first day of the week," that is the day of the discovery of Jesus' resurrection, the day on which certain of the New Testament appearance accounts transpire. Thus, at the very start of the story, Luke hints at the resurrection, surely the glorification of Christ. Moreover, Luke says that Jesus took Peter, James, and John with him up the mountain to pray. Here two more items of significance stand out. First, the mention of the mountain recalls the many Old Testament times of divine revelation that took place on mountains, so that we should not be surprised later in the story to find the voice of God addressing the disciples in a revelatory, directive manner. Second, Jesus went to pray. Luke specifies the purpose of Jesus' isolating himself in a manner consistent with his behavior throughout the Gospel. In Luke's Gospel Jesus is often at prayer, communicating with God and gaining direction and power for his work in ministry. The prayer life of Jesus is a vital part of Luke's Gospel portrait, and it provides a crucial example for the life of Jesus' disciples.

As Moses and Elijah appear with Jesus in glory, one cannot help thinking of the law and the prophets and how in Jesus the full and glorious purposes of God's work for the salvation of humanity show forth. They speak of Jesus' departure, "which he was about to accomplish in Jerusalem." Here Luke points forward to the suffering, death, resurrection, and ascension of Jesus—which together are the accomplishment of God's divine plan whereby God achieves salvation for humanity on a universal scale. The relevance of the "departure" to Jesus' forthcoming experiences in Jerusalem is reinforced by the mention of the disciples' being "weighted down with sleep." This is exactly their posture as they await the praying Jesus on the Mount of Olives. Humanity slumbers as Jesus does God's saving work for the benefit of humankind, so that the merciful work of God does for us what we cannot do for ourselves.

In the end the voice from the cloud tells the disciples who Jesus is and how they are to relate to him. As God's Son, the Chosen One through whom God accomplishes the mystery of salvation, Jesus is the one to whom disciples are to listen and, thus, obey. Luke reports that the awesome nature of the moment moved Peter, James, and John to silence. In Mark Jesus orders the restraint, but here the events themselves appear to be too much for the disciples, who still operate without full comprehension (note Peter's ignorance in this story). As the "departure" occurs later in the overall account, so the disciples' are given the power to speak of all they saw and heard in the presence of Jesus.

The Transfiguration: The Celebration

The following hymn provides a summary of the epiphanies that the Gospel lessons have been recording since the celebration of the Epiphany on January 6 until today's crucial epiphany, the Transfiguration. The first two stanzas might be sung just before the Gospel reading and the last stanza in response to it.

Songs of thankfulness and praise,
Jesus, Lord, to thee we raise,
manifested by the star
to the sages from afar;
branch of royal David's stem
in thy birth at Bethlehem;
anthems be to thee addressed,
God in flesh made manifest.

Manifest at Jordan's stream,
Prophet, Priest, and King supreme;
and at Cana, wedding-guest,
in thy Godhead manifest;
manifest in power divine,
changing water into wine;
anthems be to thee addressed,
God in flesh made manifest.

Grant us grace to see thee, Lord,
present in thy holy Word;
grace to imitate thee now
and be pure, as pure art thou;
that we may become like thee
at thy great epiphany,
and may praise thee, ever blest,
God in flesh made manifest.

(Christopher Wordsworth, altered)

A fitting tune is St. George's Windsor ("Come, Ye Thankful People Come"), with which most congregations will be familiar.

Saint Leo the Great (d. 461), preaching on the Transfiguration, had this to say about the significance of the voice from out of the cloud:

These things were said not for their profit only, who heard them with their own ears, but in these three apostles the whole Church has learned all that their eyes saw and their ears heard. Let everyone's faith then be established according to the preaching of the most holy Gospel, and let no one be ashamed of Christ's cross, through which the world was redeemed. And let not anyone fear to suffer for the cause of justice or lose confidence in the reward that has been promised.

For through toil we pass to rest and through death to life. Since all the weakness of our lowly human life was taken on by Christ, we can win the victory he has won and receive what he has promised if we continue in our faith and love for him. When it comes to obeying his commands or enduring hardships, the Father's fore-announcing voice should always be sounding in our ears, saying, "This is my beloved Son in whom I am well pleased; listen to him." (adapted from Philip Schaff and Henry Wace, eds., *A Select Library of the Nicene and Post-Nicene Fathers of the Christian Church*, vol. 12 [Grand Rapids: Eerdmans, 1956], pp. 164-65)

Scripture Index

Old Testament

New Testament

A Comparison of Major Lectionaries

YEAR C: ADVENT SUNDAY THROUGH
THE LAST SUNDAY AFTER THE EPIPHANY

	Old Testament	Psalm	Epistle	Gospel
		THE FIRST SUNDAY OF ADVENT		
RCL	Jer. 33:14-16	25:1-10	I Thess. 3:9-13	Luke 21:25-36
RoCath		25:4-5, 8-10, 14	I Thess. 3:12–4:2	Luke 21:25-28, 34-36
Episcopal	Zech. 14:4-9	50		Luke 21:25-31
Lutheran		25:1-9		
		THE SECOND SUNDAY OF ADVENT		
RCL	Baruch 5:1-9 or Malachi 3:1-4	Luke 1:68-79	Phil. 1:3-11	Luke 3:1-6
RoCath	Baruch 5:1-9	126	Phil. 1:1-6, 8-11	
Episcopal	Baruch 5:1-9	126	Phil. 1:1-11	
Lutheran	Malachi 3:1-4	126		

THE THIRD SUNDAY OF ADVENT

RCL	Zeph. 3:14-20	Isa. 12:2-6	Phil. 4:4-7	Luke 3:7-18
RoCath	Zeph. 3:14-18			Luke 3:10-18
Episcopal		or Ps. 85	Phil. 4:4-7 (8-9)	
Lutheran	Zeph. 3:14-18*a*		Phil. 4:4-7 (8-9)	

THE FOURTH SUNDAY OF ADVENT

RCL	Micah 5:2-5*a*	Luke 1:47-55 or Ps. 80:1-7	Heb. 10:5-10	Luke 1:39-45 (46-55)
RoCath	Micah 5:1-4	80:2-3, 15-16, 18-19		Luke 1:39-45
Episcopal	Micah 5:2-4	80		Luke 1:39-49 (50-56)
Lutheran	Micah 5:2-4	80:1-7		

CHRISTMAS EVE/DAY
(Third Proper)

RCL	Isa. 52:7-10	98	Heb. 1:1-4 (5-12)	John 1:1-14
RoCath		98:1-6	Heb. 1:1-6	John 1:1-18
Episcopal			Heb. 1:1-12	
Lutheran	Isa. 62:10-12		Titus 3:4-7	Luke 2:1-20

FIRST SUNDAY AFTER CHRISTMAS DAY

RCL	I Sam. 2:18-20, 26	148	Col. 3:12-17	Luke 2:41-52
RoCath	Sirach 3:2-6, 12-14	128:1-5	Col. 3:12-21	
Episcopal	Isa. 61:10–62:3	147	Gal. 3:23-25; 4:4-7	John 1:1-18
Lutheran	Jer. 31:10-13	111	Heb. 2:10-18	

NEW YEAR'S EVE/DAY

RCL	Eccl. 3:1-13	8	Rev. 21:1-6*a*	Matt. 25:31-46

RoCath Jan. 1 is observed as the Solemnity of Mary by Roman Catholics. The following lessons may be used at masses observing the beginning of the civil year, but they may not be celebrated on Jan. 1.

	Gen. 1:14-18	8:4-9 or	I Cor. 7:29-31	Matt. 6:31-34
	or Num. 6:22-27	49:2-3, 6-11, 17-18 or	or James 4:13-15	or Luke 12:35-40
		90:2-6, 12-16		

Episcopal The BCP observes Jan. 1 as the Feast of the Holy Name. See the first volume in this series for Year B.

Lutheran	Jer. 24:1-7	102:24-28	I Pet. 1:22-25	Luke 13:6-9

THE SECOND SUNDAY AFTER CHRISTMAS DAY

RCL	Jer. 31:7-14 or Sirach 24:1-12	147:12-20 or Wis. 10:15-21	Eph. 1:3-14	John 1:(1-9) 10-18
RoCath	Sirach 24:1-4, 8-12	147:12-15, 19-20	Eph. 1:3-6, 15-18	John 1:1-18
Episcopal	Jer. 31:7-14	84	Eph. 1:3-6, 15-19a	Matt. 2:13-15, 19-23 or Luke 2:41-52 or Matt. 2:1-12
Lutheran	Isa. 61:10–62:3	147:12-20	Eph. 1:3-6, 15-18	John 1:1-18

THE BAPTISM OF THE LORD
(The First Sunday after the Epiphany)

RCL	Isa. 43:1-7	29	Acts 8:14-17	Luke 3:15-17, 21-22
RoCath	Isa. 42:1-4, 6-7	29:1-4, 9c-10	Acts 10:34-38	Luke 3:15-16, 21-22
Episcopal	Isa. 42:1-9	89:1-29	Acts 10:34-38	Luke 3:15-16, 21-22
Lutheran	Isa. 42:1-7	45:7-9	Acts 10:34-38	

THE SECOND SUNDAY AFTER EPIPHANY

RCL	Isa. 62:1-5	36:5-10	I Cor. 12:1-11	John 2:1-11
RoCath		96:1-3, 7-10	I Cor. 12:4-11	John 2:1-12
Episcopal		96		
Lutheran				

THE THIRD SUNDAY AFTER EPIPHANY

RCL	Neh. 8:1-3, 5-6, 8-10	19	I Cor. 12:12-31*a*	Luke 4:14-21
RoCath	Neh. 8:2-4, 5-6, 8-10	19:8-10, 15	I Cor. 12:12-30	Luke 1:1-4; 4:14-21
Episcopal	Neh. 8:2-10	113	I Cor. 12:12-27	
Lutheran	Isa. 61:1-6	113	I Cor. 12:12-21, 26-27	

THE FOURTH SUNDAY AFTER EPIPHANY

RCL	Jer. 1:4-10	71:1-6	I Cor. 13:1-13	Luke 4:21-30
RoCath	Jer. 1:4-5, 17-19	71:1-6, 15-17	I Cor. 12:31–13:13	Luke 4:21-32
Episcopal		71:1-17	I Cor. 14:12*b*-20	Luke 4:21-32
Lutheran		71:1-6, 15-17	I Cor. 12:27–13:13	Luke 4:21-32

THE TRANSFIGURATION OF THE LORD
(The Last Sunday After Epiphany)

RCL	Exod. 34:29-35	99	II Cor. 3:12–4:2	Luke 9:28-36 (37–43)
RoCath	The Roman Catholic Church observes the Transfiguration on the Second Sunday in Lent. Today it continues to use the sequence of proper lessons for ordinary time.			
Episcopal			I Cor. 12:27–13:13	Luke 9:28-36
Lutheran	Deut. 34:1-12		II Cor. 4:3-6	Luke 9:28-36

A Liturgical Calendar

Advent Through Epiphany 1997–2007

	1997-98 C	1998-99 A	1999-2000 B	2000-01 C	2001-02 A
Advent 1	Nov. 30	Nov. 29	Nov. 28	Dec. 3	Dec. 2
Advent 2	Dec. 7	Dec. 6	Dec. 5	Dec. 10	Dec. 9
Advent 3	Dec. 14	Dec. 13	Dec. 12	Dec. 17	Dec. 16
Advent 4	Dec. 21	Dec. 20	Dec. 19	Dec. 24	Dec. 23
Christmas 1	Dec. 28	Dec. 27	Dec. 26	Dec. 31	Dec. 30
Christmas 2	Jan. 4	Jan. 3	Jan. 2	---------	Jan. 6
Epiphany 1	Jan. 11	Jan. 10	Jan. 9	Jan. 7	Jan. 13
Epiphany 2	Jan. 18	Jan. 17	Jan. 16	Jan. 14	Jan. 20
Epiphany 3	Jan. 25	Jan. 24	Jan. 23	Jan. 21	Jan. 27
Epiphany 4	Feb. 1	Jan. 31	Jan. 30	Jan. 28	Feb. 3
Epiphany 5	Feb. 8	Feb. 7	Feb. 6	Feb. 4	---------
Epiphany 6	Feb. 15	---------	Feb. 13	Feb. 11	---------
Epiphany 7	---------	---------	Feb. 20	Feb. 18	---------
Epiphany 8	---------	---------	Feb. 27	---------	---------
Last Sunday	Feb. 22	Feb. 14	Mar. 5	Feb. 25	Feb. 10

	2002-03 B	2003-04 C	2004-05 A	2005-06 B	2006-07 C
Advent 1	Dec. 1	Nov. 30	Nov. 28	Nov. 27	Dec. 3
Advent 2	Dec. 8	Dec. 7	Dec. 5	Dec. 4	Dec. 10
Advent 3	Dec. 15	Dec. 14	Dec. 12	Dec. 11	Dec. 17
Advent 4	Dec. 22	Dec. 21	Dec. 19	Dec. 18	Dec. 24
Christmas 1	Dec. 29	Dec. 28	Dec. 26	Jan. 1	Dec. 31
Christmas 2	Jan. 5	Jan. 4	Jan. 2	---------	---------
Epiphany 1	Jan. 12	Jan. 11	Jan. 9	Jan. 8	Jan. 7
Epiphany 2	Jan. 19	Jan. 18	Jan. 16	Jan. 15	Jan. 14
Epiphany 3	Jan. 26	Jan. 25	Jan. 23	Jan. 22	Jan. 21
Epiphany 4	Feb. 2	Feb. 1	Jan. 30	Jan. 29	Jan. 28
Epiphany 5	Feb. 9	Feb. 8	---------	Feb. 5	Feb. 4
Epiphany 6	Feb. 16	Feb. 15	---------	Feb. 12	Feb. 11
Epiphany 7	Feb. 23	---------	---------	Feb. 19	---------
Epiphany 8	---------	---------	---------	---------	---------
Last Sunday	Mar. 2	Feb. 22	Feb. 6	Feb. 26	Feb. 18